You and your kids can have great futures.

Your children can become emotionally healthy.

In your hands are powerful, life-changing Principles and Steps that will open up entirely new ways for you to deal with, think about, and respond to your ex.

The transformation you seek for yourself and your kids is possible.

THIS BOOK IS NOT JUST FOR PARENTS WHO ARE SEPARATED

This book is for anyone who cares about, or is close to, separated parents and their children.

Parents, grandparents, relatives, guardians, caregivers, friends, counselors, and educators all can help to bring much needed stability and guidance into the lives of exes and their children using these Principles and Steps.

PARENT WARS

Dealing With An Ex

To Build Emotionally Healthy Kids

Dr. Donald R. Partridge

pear
PUBLISHING
San Francisco Bay Area

PARENT WARS
Dealing With An Ex
To Build Emotionally Healthy Kids
Dr. Donald R. Partridge

Pear Publishing, Inc.
Post Office Box 10092
Pleasanton, CA 94588-2747
Website: www.pearpublishing.net
E-mail: info@pearpublishing.net

ISBN-10 (Print version): 1-940824-04-4
ISBN-13 (Print version): 978-1-940824-04-8
         (ePUB version): 978-1-940824-01-7
         (ePDF version): 978-1-940824-02-4

Library of Congress Control Number: 2014912614

First Edition 2015. Printed and bound in the United States of America.

10 9 8 7 6 5 4 3 2 1

Cover design: Bo Lane, Vancouver, WA
Interior Book Design: One-on-One Book Production, West Hills, CA
Illustrations: Designior, Pleasanton, CA
Disclaimer: G. Miller Hogan II, J.D., Nashville, TN
Author photo: Clyde Brewster, Pleasanton, CA

To my daughter and son

DISCLAIMER

This is my story. The events described in this book are my version and my beliefs about the events that have taken place in my life and in the lives of my children and my ex-wife. I have made every effort to be as accurate as possible, but also know that with the emotions and complexities of separation and divorce different participants may perceive the events described herein differently. There are two sides to every issue and in this book I am only representing my own response to the events that I describe. My ex-wife, her second husband, and the other persons who are mentioned (but not named) in this book may have different responses. I am only able to relate my perspective and my interpretation of those events. It is my intent to recount the facts as I recall them and my own personal emotions and feelings in reaction to those events.

The events described in this book are included solely for the purpose of providing the reader with the context necessary to examine and contemplate the effects that Parent Wars have on children who experience parent separation.

Apart from the author's personal stories in this book, the additional stories, anecdotes, and narratives are compilations of multiple stories the author has collected over the past twenty years, or, stories heard repeatedly by the author—each story coming with its own setting, gender, and age. Therefore, regarding the additional stories, no one particular story can be attributable to any one specific individual or family.

Neither the publisher nor the author is engaged in rendering medical, psychological, or any other kind of personal or professional services or therapy. Readers should consult their own medical, psychological, or other competent professional before adopting any of the concepts in this book or drawing inferences from it. The content of this book is general, whereas each reader's situation is unique. Therefore, as with all books of this nature, the purpose is to provide general information rather than address individual situations.

The author and publisher specifically disclaim all responsibility for any liability, loss, or risk, personal or otherwise, which is incurred as a consequence, directly or indirectly, of the use and application of the contents of this book.

CONTENTS

PART 3 TRIUMPH

ABUSE

Abuse in any form is never tolerated. The Principles and Steps discussed in this book in no way suggest that parents or children are ever to be placed in harm's way.

WHAT YOU ARE ABOUT TO READ

PART 1: TRAUMA

The progressive hollowing out of our daughter through our Parent Wars...

How my ex and I took our innocent young daughter and destroyed her emotionally, making it impossible for her to make good decisions, forcing her into years of self-destructive behaviors

PART 2: TRANSITION

The introduction of some life-changing, revolutionary Principles and Steps that will alter the ways to deal with an ex—resulting in incredible emotional health for kids

PART 3: TRIUMPH

The incredible restoration of my daughter to making good decisions, to healthy behaviors, and to emotional stability

PART 1

TRAUMA

The progressive hollowing out of our daughter
through our Parent Wars…

How my ex and I took our innocent young daughter and
destroyed her emotionally, making it impossible for
her to make good decisions, forcing her into years of
self-destructive behaviors

WHEN EVERYTHING WENT WRONG

My phone rang.

I looked to see who was calling and suddenly a black cloud came over me.

It was my ex.

Why was she calling? I hated that woman.

All she said was that our daughter had run away again and that this time nobody knew where she was. Then she hung up.

I sat there stunned, staring at my phone.

So that was it. My poor daughter. Her behavior had been spiraling downhill for years—defiant, rebellious, and untamable. She had run away before but nothing like this. She had finally hit bottom. My fifteen-year-old was now completely gone.

I blamed her mother.

Years earlier, my ex left our marriage saying to me that she wanted to discover a new life for herself and new relationships.

I was convinced she had little regard for our children, believing she was ignoring the emotional damage she was causing them by her choice of lifestyle.

Back then I couldn't just stand there and let my kids think their mother's behavior was acceptable—so I fought back. I taught my children to oppose their mother. I wanted them to know the truth about her. I wanted them to object to her behavior. I wanted them to favor loyalty and faithfulness. I wanted them to favor me.

But their mother also vigorously opposed me.

It was too much for my kids, causing them serious emotional problems, especially my daughter.

I hated everything about my ex.

I hated everything about my ex.

Does any of this sound familiar?

Is there anything in this story that you might identify with?

Once separation occurs, everything—and it seems like everyone—changes. Everyone is affected, especially the kids.

The connection with our exes once built on companionship and trust is now filled with broken promises and painful memories, and for many of us, feelings of betrayal and deceit.

Now, just to see the ex is difficult. Just hearing their name or talking about them is hard. I know many parents who still, after several years, cannot bear to say the name of their ex.

Once we couldn't live without these individuals. Now when we see them, we're filled with all this emotional heaviness.

Some of us wish our exes would just go away. What a dream come true if we never saw or had any dealings with them again. But because of our children we find ourselves bound to the other parent in ways we cannot escape.

Some of us wish our exes would just go away.

And we're extremely concerned for our kids.

There seems to be no end to their troubles and complications. Our children have been deeply affected by our separation and continue to suffer.

And we're worried about the influence of the other parent on our children. Some of us dread it when our kids are over at the other house. We disagree with the way our ex is raising our kids, how they're being dressed, what they eat, and how they are—or are not—disciplined.

But what may bother us the most are the new lifestyles and philosophies of our exes. We want our kids to listen to us and follow our example and how we do things. Like one mom said when seeing her kids after six weeks with their father, "For the first few days I hardly knew them. Their mannerisms and the way they talked shocked me."

And then there's the ex's new dating partner! Don't get me started!

Some relationships may be fine, but for the most part the partners are worse than the ex. And we've seen a change come over our ex since the new relationship. Where once the ex was fairly agreeable, now there are all these walls and roadblocks. And our kids are taking the brunt of the difficulties. With the arrival of the new partner, our children are confronted with new relationships and complicated emotions. And we are powerless to do anything about it. The terrible realization hits us: Strangers are raising—or influencing—our kids!

The terrible realization hits us:
Strangers are raising—or influencing—our kids!

If your ex has left you…

You bear the terrible anguish of feeling betrayed and

rejected. But you also carry the agonizing knowledge that your ex is happy with the separation, active with their new partner, loving their new lifestyles, enjoying the freedom of being a part-time parent, and living the life they say they always wanted. But you're left to suffer terribly, to bear the humiliation of being alone, to agonize at being separated from your kids, and to carry the burden of raising them with far fewer resources and finances.

Or, if you're the one who left the marriage or the relationship...

You may have done so because you were tired of the deceit, the lying, the irresponsibility, and the immaturity. You felt as if you were emotionally underwater with no way out.

Or, you just found somebody else. What was once a loving relationship with your former partner evaporated long ago, leaving you isolated with no prospects of future happiness.

Now, since your departure, your ex has become extremely critical, refuses to let go of the past, and continues to be at war against you—and nobody seems to take your side or even wants to hear what you have to say. Everyone is siding with your ex. Your ex's slander and lies about you have influenced friends and relatives against you and have deeply stigmatized you. Your ex seems to be getting more benefit, more sympathy, and more favor than you.

The worst thing about your separation is that your ex has turned your children against you. But you're also a faithful parent. You love your kids too. Yet your ex has criticized you to your kids, kept your children from you, trained them to withdraw from you, has taken every opportunity to speak against you, and has shown disgust whenever your name is mentioned. And it has worked. Now, between you and your children there is an emotional wall, with your children becoming more and more detached. What you hoped would have been an amicable separation has spun completely out of control—the other parent and your children are siding against you.

The worst thing about your separation is that your ex has turned your children against you.

For all of us...

Communicating with our ex is like communicating with an enemy. Every conversation comes with heaviness and difficulty. Our ex is non-responsive, resists our helpful comments, and continues to be insulting. Everything has become deadlocked. Just coming to a simple agreement is nearly impossible. It may take us days to recover emotionally from conversations with our ex.

The whole system of parent separation is painful. It's like walking in lead boots. Everything associated with an ex is miserable, labor-intensive, and heavy.

I know about all of this.

I've personally experienced it all.

I, too, am a separated parent.

MY SEPARATION

I thought I was happily married.

I never gave it a thought when my wife began working late several evenings a week. She said it was a requirement of her job.

I still didn't get it when my wife sat me down one evening and told me that she wanted a new life. I seriously thought she was talking about remodeling the kitchen or something. She finally got through to me that the new life she wanted included everything but me.

She told me our marriage was over and that tonight she wanted us to separate.

I was in complete shock. This couldn't be happening. Things like this happened to others but not to me. And not to us! We've been happily married for twelve years, right? And we have two incredible kids. How can she do this?

I never knew a human being could be in as much pain as I was that night.

I was devastated. She was overjoyed. I was forced into a world of indescribable anguish and personal loneliness. Her world was filled with exploration and thrills. She had entered some sort of heaven. I had just been thrown into hell.

She had entered some sort of heaven.
I had just been thrown into hell.

During the months that followed I could not accept the fact that I was a separated parent. I was convinced that our separation was only temporary. "Tonight," I would think, "I'll get the call. Tonight she will certainly miss her kids and me and will want to come home."

I became a doormat, agreeable to almost anything. I became the best ex-spouse in the world—anything to win her back.

I was also the most naïve ex-spouse in the world.

There were times my ex and I would have a great phone conversation and I would think, "This is it! She's coming back!"

But then, as it always happened, she'd ask for some favor—could I pay a certain bill or take the kids on her weekend. I, of course, would pay whatever she asked or keep the kids. We were rebuilding, right? I was very careful not to cause any problems between us.

But then, nothing. I would hear nothing from her. Later my kids would say something about mom going off with 'Bill' for a weekend.

My heart would break. It would take me days just to breathe normally again. Once more I was forced to realize our 'great' conversation was just a ploy to get what she wanted. I admit it. I realized that I was a fool and had allowed myself to be sucked in every time. But my belief in her and my belief in the restoration of our marriage continued to dominate my thinking. I'm ashamed to say that this went on for nearly two years.

But after the fortieth time (or was it the hundredth time?) I finally got the message. I finally woke up to the fact that the only reason she was ever nice was when she wanted something. I mean, what did it take? I realized at last that our relationship was really over and had been since the day she announced she wanted out. So I finally stopped believing in her. And I stopped believing she would come back.

Two years after we separated I let our marriage go. It was the most miserable day of my life.

Any positive feelings I had about her instantly evaporated.

And I was surprised how quickly I turned against her.

I loathed her. I despised her. I hated her for forcing me to be a separated parent, for making me live alone, for breaking my heart and the hearts of our children. I hated her for what I felt was her betrayal and for what I saw as her disloyalty and dishonesty. I hated her for taking advantage of my kindness and using me for the past two years.

I now believed my ex was the worst person to ever walk the face of the planet.

I wanted nothing to do with her. I never wanted to see her again or hear her name. I wished she were out of my life and out of my kids' lives forever.

I was surprised how quickly I turned against her.

Then an idea came to me. If my children were to reject their mother, we could all be free from this woman—whom I considered evil.

Here was a real possibility and one that I began to pursue.

I was no longer a good ex-spouse.

PARENT WAR 1: LOSING PRIMARY CUSTODY OF MY DAUGHTER

When I remarried, my second wife and I blended our marriage with her three children and my two. Her two youngest were the same ages as my two. With both of us having primary custody of our kids they all spent a lot of time together and became best friends. And my children loved their stepmother. As far as I was concerned, my second wife quickly became the real mother to my children. She is a woman of character who loved my kids and we were one big happy family. I thought to myself: Who needed the worthless biological mother anyway?

My new-found happiness wasn't lost on my ex.

When my kids were with their mother, I knew she had to sit through story after story about their new family and all of the wonderful things going on over at my house. Hey, I had endured years of the stories about their mother going out with all her dating partners, so I hoped her hearing my stories made her just as miserable.

It did.

Over the phone my ex screamed at me about my new family, my new home, and my 'wonderful' new life, accusing me of trying to cut her out of our kids' lives. In no uncertain terms she told me that she was the only mother to our two children and that she wanted her kids back immediately.

I told her to get lost.

I asked her to tell me who has been the responsible parent the past several years, who has been faithful, and who has set a good example for our children? Not her. She barely saw them. I told her she no longer deserved to be my children's mother. I told her she didn't love our children. Acting the way she did, how could she? Her lifestyle I detested. I told her she was incapable of contributing anything to the well-being of our children. I told her she was replaceable and that she should be replaced.

The gloves were off.

My ex declared war.

I returned her rage with full force.

My ex declared war. I returned her rage with full force.

Our attorney met with my new wife and me at our house. After observing for himself our comfortable home, our child-friendly neighborhood, our children happily playing together, and their excellent private schools, he shook his head and said that there was no way under heaven that the courts would ever take my children from me.

Another attorney also resolutely agreed. This attorney strongly maintained that my ex's demand for a change in custody was nothing more than frivolous. And, experts in the field basically said the same thing—that the lawsuit would be easily defeated because the court does not favor removing children from established homes where they are thriving.

So the court assigned us a mediator who was to interview my children's mother and me, assess our situations, and make a recommendation to the court regarding custody arrangements. We also learned that even though mediators only make recommendations, they are most often accepted verbatim by the judge. The recommendations could be challenged, but to do so would require a lengthy legal process and could become extremely expensive. And, such challenges rarely succeed.

Up to this point my new family and I had been living together in a small home but we were now able with our combined incomes to purchase a larger home. We were hesitant to proceed because of the child-custody lawsuit looming over us. Yet, because of the assurances of two family attorneys and several experts we decided to go ahead with our plans to put our home up for sale and look for a new home.

A couple of months later everything came together over one weekend. On a Sunday we accepted an offer for the sale of our home and also filled out papers for the purchase of our new dream home.

But the very next day my attorney called to tell me he had just received the recommendation of the court mediator. He was so shocked he had difficulty talking. With a halting voice he told me that the mother had won. The mediator's recommendation, he said, was that primary custody of both my children was to go to their mother.

With a halting voice he told me that the mother had won.

I sat there in shock, barely able to hold the phone. How could this mediator make such a mistake? What about all the assurances of every professional I had ever spoken with? I was overwhelmed with emotion.

With a heavy voice the attorney told me he was absolutely appalled and that in all his years of practice he had never seen a recommendation so completely unwarranted. I was at a loss for words. What could I do? He suggested that we appeal the recommendation before a judge. He said it would be expensive and take some time, but a judge would certainly issue a far more reasonable and fair judgment than the mediator had done.

I said that I was willing to begin. "Let's fight this thing," I replied. "Let's begin the appeal."

Once off the phone, I left work. I called my wife and we both wept.

I then called one of the experts who had heard the news and who was also deeply dismayed.

In his office that day I repeatedly asked him why I had lost my case. Why did my ex get custody of my children? How could she possibly have won? Hadn't he assured me that hers was a frivolous lawsuit and that there was no way I could lose?

Finally, shaking his head in distress, he said quietly, "The mediator is unqualified."

I said, "Unqualified? What are you talking about?"

Choosing each word very carefully he said almost in a whisper that his colleagues and he were convinced even before this mediator was assigned my case that this mediator was inexperienced. He told me that the recommendation should never have favored my ex-wife.

I was stunned.

He was disgusted.

This expert was very sorry for me, but his sorrow couldn't hold a candle to mine. Because of this so-called inexperienced and unqualified mediator, I was about to lose my two children.

Because of this so-called inexperienced and unqualified mediator, I was about to lose my two children.

My wife and I realized that if I lost my appeal and my ex

were to take my children, she would undoubtedly sue for the highest possible amount of child support. We would not be able to make payments on a new home and child support as well. So, late that evening I called our realtor, retracted our offer to purchase the new home, and cancelled the sale of our current home. Our dream home would just have to wait.

My attorney and I did file to overturn the mediator's recommendation, but it was like walking in sand. The process took months. Finally we were scheduled to talk informally with a judge who wanted to help us reach a settlement to keep us from having to go to court.

While waiting to see the judge, my ex and her attorney sat on one side of a large lobby area while my attorney and I sat on the other side. Suddenly into the lobby came our mediator. Recognizing my ex, the mediator lit up, all smiles, and went directly over to her. They hugged each other and stood there laughing and talking together for quite some time. The mediator then looked over in my direction, and when our eyes met, stopped smiling, didn't say a word, and walked out of the room. What was to me a clear display of favoritism and lack of professionalism was sickening.

After meeting with us and hearing our stories, the judge recommended, as a way of settlement, that my daughter would live with the mother but my son would remain with me. We would arrange child visitation so that our children would spend every weekend together.

What was to me a clear display of favoritism and lack of professionalism was sickening.

I accepted the recommendation but was profoundly distressed knowing this was the best I could do. And, I was deeply grieved. I was about to lose my precious daughter—I couldn't imagine daily life without her.

So, Parent War 1 was over.

It didn't take long to figure out what was going to happen next. My ex didn't waste any time.

PARENT WAR 2: LOSING PRIMARY CUSTODY OF MY SON

A few weeks after the first Parent War, my wife and I were out for a walk when suddenly a man ran toward us and, running directly into me, shoved papers into my hands. His aggressive physical actions frightened my wife. A bit shocked, we watched as he then ran across the street and hopped into a car driven by my ex-wife's new husband and they sped away. I discovered that I had been served with court papers informing me that my ex was now suing for custody of my son.

I was absolutely devastated. We had just completed a year and a half of hostile litigation over my daughter and now we were being forced to go back into court and back into more court-ordered mediation. This time, fortunately, we had a different mediator, not the one I considered so disastrous on our first case.

My defense against my ex was I believed that she was an unfit mother, that she was the one who had abandoned the family, and that I was the one who had provided the stability my children so desperately needed following their mother's desertion. In my mind I had a proven record but all she had were words and empty promises.

But in her favor my ex had our daughter living with her and the momentum of her past victory. As the days dragged into weeks, I was consumed by this second Parent War. I was miserable that my daughter no longer lived with me, and now I was overwhelmed with the real possibility of losing my son. Over and over I rehearsed the unfairness of it all.

I was overwhelmed with the real possibility of losing my son.
Over and over I rehearsed the unfairness of it all.

At our first meeting with the mediator my ex came out swinging. The hostility she displayed was over the top. Her accusations were outrageous. She told the mediator that I had abused my children, that I was completely insensitive to their needs, and that she feared for their health and safety. She accused me of brainwashing them, teaching them strange religious practices, and indoctrinating them into seditious and subversive behaviors and thoughts.

What a pack of lies! To me the facts were clear for anyone to see: After her desertion I was the one who raised our children while she went out and played. Who got the kids ready for school? Who picked them up after school? Who helped them with their homework? Who fed them, clothed them, and took them to sports? Who was with them for months on end? Who wasn't with them? Who was off with dating partners? Who couldn't even maintain a regular visitation schedule to see her children?

Yes, my children went to a highly reputable private school, and yes, my children went to a neighborhood church on Sunday mornings. If that was brainwashing my kids and if that was strange religious practices, then that showed how out of touch she was. Both of my kids were well-dressed, well-behaved, and did well in school. How could she possibly accuse me of neglecting them?

The mediator just sat there looking at us. For over an hour he listened to our blistering accusations, our bitter animosity, and our complete inability to agree on anything. It was clear to him that my ex and I hated everything about each other.

Finally he spoke. Sitting up straight in his chair he pointed to a file folder about three inches thick. He told us that file contained details of our last custody battle which had lasted well over eighteen months. He was sickened by us as parents and appalled at our complete lack of ability to work together on behalf of our children. He said he was so ashamed of us that he could barely stand to be in the same room with us.

"And now look at you!" he exclaimed. "You're going into another prolonged custody battle over your son!" Pointing his finger at both of us he told us in no uncertain terms that we were to stop this custody battle today. With as much force as he could muster he told us that the damage of a prolonged war to our children was unimaginable. He said he didn't care whether my son lived with me or his mother but that this battle was to stop immediately and that we were going into resolution right now.

The mediator's message was crystal clear. And I knew he was right. I looked at my ex to see her reaction. She was sitting there stone cold. She didn't appear to be moved in the slightest by the mediator's speech. It was very clear that I was in for another long drawn-out court battle.

---

*It was very clear that I was in for another
long drawn-out court battle.*

After a long silence, with the mediator sitting there glaring at both of us, with resignation I said, "I guess it's on me to make the decision."

I believed the mediator. Another war would devastate our

kids. But this was killing me. Was I to give up my son? How could I do such a thing? But for the sake of the kids, what else could I do?

Another long silence.

I threw in the towel.

I couldn't believe the words coming out of my mouth. I told the mediator it was over, that she could have my son. I asked as a way of settlement that I would get the majority of the weekends each month with both children.

It was absolutely the worst day of my life.

I had thought the divorce was bad, but it was nothing compared to what was happening now. I was overcome with grief. In both custody battles I had been the one to give in. Why hadn't I been able to go the distance in my opposition to my former wife? Why couldn't I endure the conflicts? Why couldn't I stand up against the recommendations of the mediators? Why couldn't I finally get my case before a formal judge in court?

I hated the decision, I hated the court system, and I hated myself.

I asked myself, why couldn't the mediators see through this woman? Why were they rewarding what I saw as her betrayal of my children and her selfishness? They seemed to scoff at my faithfulness and commitment to my kids. Why was my devotion to my children mocked by my ex and counted as nothing by the court? She couldn't even fulfill her weekend visitation schedule. Why was my having to pick up her slack considered meaningless? Why didn't anyone appreciate that I never left my kids?

I hated the decision, I hated the court system, and I hated myself.

The months following the loss of my children were sheer torment. Gone were the evenings helping with homework, gone were the meals with all of us sitting around telling stories, gone were the long periods of time just hanging out with both of them. I couldn't wait until the weekends. Even the weekends when I didn't have the kids, I'd drive down to watch them play sports. I did everything I could to be near them.

But things only got worse! As both of my children spent time with their mother, they began to change. Their demeanor changed. They dressed differently. They even talked differently. I wanted my children to be normal, wear normal clothes, look like normal kids, have normal friends, make good grades, and live normal lives. But their mother wouldn't have it. As a 'free spirit' she made up special haircuts for my children, shaving one side of my seven-year-old daughter's head, and dressing her in clothes I thought were inappropriate even for a twenty-year-old.

I couldn't believe that my children were moving in such a heartbreaking direction. This wasn't what I wanted for them, and the thought of them living the rest of their childhood away from me was unbearable.

PARENT WAR 3: MY EX AFTER MORE MONEY

"You might as well give up, Don," her voice on the phone blared into my ear. It was my ex, the voice I hated. She had recently taken to taunting me. I had just been subpoenaed for a third time to appear in family court. This time my ex was after more child-support money.

Her mocking continued. "Every time we go to litigation, I win. You've lost both times before, and you're going to lose again. You may as well give it up—don't even bother. The court's on my side."

Her arrogance was nauseating.

Her mocking continued. "Every time we go to litigation, I win."

I now viewed my ex as little more than human wreckage, a once-promising woman gone totally wrong.

I had bought a one-hour consultation with an attorney to discuss the latest volley from my ex. It was an hour well spent. Because it was my second wife's income that had substantially increased in recent months and not mine, the lawyer said that the court was not likely to rule in my ex's favor.

So I decided to save attorney's fees by representing myself. My ex, meanwhile, retained an expensive attorney, and I soon discovered a clever way to strike back at her. I called her attorney frequently—every day, sometimes two or three times a day. If I had a question about a litigation point, I was on the phone. If the question was about some legal procedure, I made the call. If I needed financial data, a legal definition, even a recommendation for a good place for lunch, I called her attorney.

My frequent calls were costing my ex a small fortune. Payback! I had finally found some means of getting back at her, a legitimate way to hurt her. She had so dismantled me emotionally, taking away my children and now suing for more money. I had no way to oppose her, no way of causing her even a small amount of the misery she had caused me. But now I had found a way. I knew it was trivial compared to what she had done to me, but it was something. And I used it to full advantage.

I wanted to wound her. I wanted to hit her where it hurt—in this case, right in her bank account. At last, I was the one to inflict pain instead of being on the receiving end. It felt so good. And just as I suspected, the court ruled that I did not owe my ex any additional money.

I won. Ha.

It felt great. Where was her boasting now? Why wasn't she calling me to taunt me now? Just imagining what it cost her to sue me gave me incredible delight.

I HATED MY EX

All during our Parent Wars it would grind me emotionally to hear anything positive about my ex.

I couldn't stand to hear that she was happy. And unfortunately for me, things were going well for her. She was living a pretty good life. She had remarried, had two more kids, lived in a nice home, drove a nice car, and wore nice clothes. This flew in the face of my sense of justice. How could she forsake a marriage, mess up our kids, ruin my life, and come out doing so well? To me it made values like faithfulness, honesty, commitment, and self-sacrifice meaningless.

So I recruited my children to join with me in my wars against their mother—and it worked. My critical attitudes became their critical attitudes. My objections became their objections.

Her continual failings gave me the opportunity to encourage my children's criticisms and growing disrespect for her. When she was late, or didn't do what she promised to do, or neglected to help them with their homework, or forgot an orthodontia appointment, my kids heard about it. I was also helpful to point out additional irresponsible behaviors they didn't even know about.

My children would voice their complaints to their mother causing huge arguments between them—even between the mother and stepfather.

I was on to something good.

Her continual failings gave me the opportunity to encourage my children's criticisms and growing disrespect for her.

Even the media helped me out.

What movies don't include stories of unfaithfulness and deceit? And what week goes by without a celebrity or sports figure leaving his or her spouse for someone else? Before me were unlimited examples to remind my children about their mother.

"Do you know that woman left her husband for another man? I wonder how her kids feel."

"She says she's free to explore new relationships. I wonder what her husband and kids think?"

"Where did she get all that money? Look at how she's dressed. I bet she spends all her child support money on herself. It's supposed to be for her kids."

My children knew who I was talking about. But hey, if the shoe fits....

I also opposed their mother in more subtle ways: through silence or just changing the subject.

When I would pick up my kids from their mom's house, they'd be all excited to tell me about events of the past week. But I, of course, cut off all discussions:

"Hey dad, we went camping last weekend. It was a blast." Silence.

"Dad, we got a new kitty last week. She's so cute." I didn't want to know.

"Dad. You won't believe this. Last week we won a gold medal in ice skating and mom and I climbed Mt. Everest."

"Yeah, okay. Put your backpacks upstairs in your bedrooms and come down for dinner."

Was I harsh, angry, and somewhat out of control? Were my actions toward my ex disturbing?

At the time I believed every opposition and every negative opinion I had toward my ex was completely justified. In fact, I felt it was wrong of me to do anything other than fully oppose that woman.

PARENT WAR 4: DIFFICULTIES WITH THE STEPFATHER

My thirteen-year-old daughter climbed into the passenger seat to begin her weekend with me and began sobbing. I asked her what was wrong.

She said, "My stepdad scares me. I'm afraid he's going to hurt me."

I immediately reacted. "Has he ever hurt you?"

"No. But he makes us stand at attention like we're in the Army or something, and screams at my brother and me with his face right in our faces. All we are allowed to say is 'Yes sir.' It scares me so much. And then he got so mad at me that he threw a table against some chairs and broke everything. Dad, I'm scared of him. I'm scared he might hurt me."

"My stepdad scares me. I'm afraid he's going to hurt me."

I had known from the time he moved in with my children's mother that the stepdad was hard on my kids. I had heard from my son how he would become intensely angry with him and his sister, regularly lining them up and yelling at them. My kids had said they often had to tiptoe around their stepfather and avoid being in the same room with him because of his explosive anger.

But now this stepdad had crossed the line.

Threatening my children and breaking things in front of them was outrageous. How dare he treat my son and daughter like that! How dare their mother allow her husband to frighten my children!

It would become our fourth Parent War. And this time I was the one to bring it on.

I filed for a change in custody and believed I had an airtight case. Finally I could prove what was really going on over at that other household.

Because of her age—thirteen—my daughter could clearly describe in detail the treatment she and her brother were subjected to by their stepdad. I was convinced that all she had to do was to tell the court what she had told me and a change of primary custody was guaranteed.

I assured my daughter that she was going to soon speak with someone who was really nice, and I emphasized that it was important for her to tell this person everything she told me.

"Just tell the truth," I would tell my daughter. "Just tell the mediator how your stepfather screams at you and your brother with his face inches from yours, how he breaks things in front of you to scare you, that you are afraid for your own personal safety, and that your mother stands by doing nothing to help."

My daughter was completely agreeable and assured me she would be up-front and honest with the mediator.

I was overjoyed. No way was I going to lose this case.

I couldn't help daydreaming about my kids back home with me. Once I got my daughter back, the door would be open to pursue getting my son. It was thrilling to me that I was on the verge of having my kids once again living with me.

Finally the day arrived to meet with the court mediator— another mediator, new to us—who planned to speak to all of us individually: first my daughter, then her mother, then me.

My daughter arrived with her mother and we all sat together in the waiting room. Not a word was spoken between us.

Glancing at the mother I thought to myself, "Lady, you're going down. The truth will now be told about you and your husband's atrocious treatment of my children. I hope they're taken away from you and you never see them again."

"Lady, you're going down. The truth will now be told..."

My daughter was called in first. The interview lasted twenty minutes and then she was asked to go sit in a separate room by herself. My ex was called in next. After twenty minutes with the mediator she was asked to join our daughter in that same private room. I was left alone in the waiting room.

Now it was my turn.

I was shocked at the mediator's abruptness. Her voice and body language clearly communicated her disgust with me. I felt as if I were the one on trial. She asked me why I brought on the lawsuit. I told her about my daughter's difficulties with her stepfather and that she was afraid for her personal safety. Standing up, the mediator said that the meeting was over and that I was to have a seat back in the waiting room to wait for her written recommendation.

Back in the waiting room I sat there alone and dumbfounded.

My heart was on the ground.

Why the abruptness? Why the hostility against me? Why twenty minutes with my daughter, then twenty minutes with her mother, but only minutes with me?

Why the abruptness? Why the hostility against me?

The mediator didn't take long. Without saying a word she walked into the waiting room, handed me her recommendation, turned her back on me, and left.

Her evaluation said that my custody suit against my ex was frivolous, that the problems my daughter was experiencing at her mom's house were not because of my ex or her husband but because of me—that I was the troublemaker, that primary custody would remain with the mother, and that the visitation I currently had with both my daughter and son was to be cut in half effective immediately.

I couldn't believe what I was reading.

I was the troublemaker? My complaints against the stepdad and my daughter's mother were frivolous? My actions were distressing my daughter and son? And my visitation was now to be cut in half?

How incomprehensibly wrong. What an outrage. The injustice was unbelievable.

I was trying to save my daughter from what I believed was an unsafe household—yet I was the one being punished and the one to be silenced.

I was trying to save my daughter from what I believed was an unsafe household—yet I was the one being punished...

As I continued thinking about the completely backward recommendation of the mediator, I came to the realization that my daughter must have changed her story.

I became convinced that she had clammed up. If my daughter had told the mediator the truth, there was no way the mediator would have ruled against me.

And, I later learned that this was exactly what happened.

My daughter's interview with the mediator went something like this:

The mediator asked my daughter how things were going over at her mother's house.

"Fine," she replied.

"Are there any difficulties between you and your stepfather?"

"No."

"Do your mother and stepfather seem to have any problems?"

"No."

"Would you prefer to live with your father?"

"No."

"Is it true that your stepdad has broken things in front of you and scared you?"

"No."

It would be three years later, during a conversation with my son, when I would learn the awful and heartbreaking reasons why my daughter changed her story and why she didn't tell the truth.

After the mediator's recommendation, in the car back to her mother's house, my daughter's mother told our daughter I was mad at her for betraying me and that I didn't want to ever see her again.

My daughter was already feeling terribly guilty over her silence with the mediator. She knew she had let me down and knew that she was the reason why I had lost my case. Now, believing her mother's lies about me, my daughter was convinced that she had caused me to hate her.

Throughout her life I had been my daughter's rock and support, but now with our relationship in shreds, it literally destroyed her emotionally.

---

*Now, believing her mother's lies about me, my daughter
was convinced that she had caused me to hate her.*

But this was only the beginning of her hardships.

Emboldened by their success in court, even more pressure was put on my daughter by her mother and stepfather. My daughter said that when lining her up to be punished her stepfather would mock her and yell into her face, "Are you going to tell your father? Are you going to run off to your dad? He lost in court and you have nowhere else to go. He doesn't even want to see you." And her mother made sure she never forgot that she had betrayed her to me.

So here was my daughter, just a young teenager, isolated and cornered, knowing she had failed me in court, jeered at by her stepfather, belittled by her mother, and convinced that she had lost me as a father.

My lawsuit put my daughter in a box from which she could not escape. No matter what she said she would have betrayed a parent. If she had told the truth, she would have betrayed her mother. If she didn't tell the truth, she would have betrayed me.

The expectations put on my daughter were too much for her. She was only thirteen years old but expected to respond in a way that would have been difficult for a thirty-year-old. The lawsuit set her up for the worst kind of failure, a failure that divided her from her mother and me, and a failure that tore directly into her soul.

So in a very sick sense our work was complete.

My ex and I had taken a precious, innocent, trusting, beautiful young girl, our only daughter, and hollowed her out.

Gone were my daughter's childlike exuberance and confidence and innocence; in their place were fear, confusion, rejection, and shame.

My ex and I had taken a precious, innocent, trusting, beautiful young girl, our only daughter, and hollowed her out.

By constantly slandering each other and hounding our daughter to take sides, her mother and I had torn away the very fabric of her young life, decimating her ability to be normal and innocent. All she wanted was to live with the assurance that she was deeply loved by both parents, and to love both of her parents. Instead we forced this sweet thirteen-year-old into the dark side of an adult world—a world of pain and brokenness, hatred and animosity, bitterness and treachery—a world in which mature adults can barely function, let alone a young girl still in her formative years.

It was all too much for her. The very two individuals who should have given her security and confidence removed it from her. My daughter spun off completely, turning against everything she once valued. Because she saw herself as a failure—believing she was a disappointment to her mother and me—she decided to avoid both of us. She rarely stayed at her mom's home, living instead with friends, out all hours of the day and night, and to the mom's delight staying as far away from me as possible. When I'd come pick up my son, my daughter was conveniently absent.

I saw her sporadically over the next couple of years. It was heartbreaking to watch her behavior go downhill. And, the more my daughter's behavior declined the more she withdrew from me. Finally, several months went by in which I didn't see her at all.

The next time I saw her, I would barely recognize her.

The next time I saw her, I would barely recognize her.

PARENT WAR 5: MY DAUGHTER IN A LOCKED-DOWN FACILITY

By this time I was determined to never set foot in a courtroom against my ex again. Litigation against her was futile and I was done. Every encounter I had with mediators was disastrous—every time they bought completely into what the mother had to say against me. It was hopeless. I had thrown in the towel and accepted the fact that my children were with their mother until adulthood.

But my kids had other plans.

My phone rang showing a number I didn't recognize. I answered and I heard my daughter's pleading voice, "Dad, I need help." I was both shocked to hear her voice and thrilled that she was calling me. But the tone of her voice told me that she was in serious trouble.

Without waiting for my reply she continued, "I can't live there anymore. I just can't live there." By 'there,' of course, she meant her mother's house. I quickly learned that during the months I had not seen her, her behavior toward her mother and stepfather had changed dramatically. Instead of being passive in the face of her stepfather's tirades, she had begun fighting back. All the frustration and bitterness and anger inside my daughter were released on her mother and her stepdad—scream for scream, hate for hate. And now, she had run away.

I drove immediately to pick her up at her friend's house where she was staying.

"Dad, I have nowhere to go," said my daughter when she got into my car. "I can't go home to mom's house. I can't do it anymore. I hate it there. They constantly criticize me and yell at me. My stepdad's worse than ever. Most of the time he won't say a word to me but just walks around acting angry and slamming things. And if he does speak, he screams at me. He rages at me all the time and I hate it. It's the same way with mom. The only time she speaks to me is to yell at me, and she tells me that I'm worthless and will never make her happy. Dad, it's so terrible at my mom's house I had to run away. But now my girlfriend's parents are kicking me out and I have nowhere else to go."

As my daughter was talking to me through her tears, I could barely concentrate on what she was saying because I was so shocked at her appearance. Was this really my daughter? It sounded like her. But it didn't look like her. Yes, this was my daughter, but what had happened to her? Look at her hair. Look how she is dressed. Listen to how she talks!

I decided to take her to my home so that we could sort things out, but I knew this would put me in serious trouble with her mom. If the mom knew I was harboring my daughter, she would pursue me as a criminal in court. There was no way I could keep my daughter with me. At my house we both agreed that the only thing we could do was take her back to her mom's. She sat there resigned to her fate. She knew how she would be treated once she got home. I now had a glimpse of my daughter's world, and it was too horrible to grasp. I was absolutely unable to help her. It would be futile to try again in the court.

I now had a glimpse of my daughter's world,
and it was too horrible to grasp.

When we arrived at the house, I could see her mother's fury and hatred toward me—and toward our daughter.

Through my daughter I learned that her mother and stepfather could not stand the fact that I had again become aware of problems in their home. It made them insanely furious at her. And she would have to pay the price.

"Get inside this instant," the mother said to our daughter.

Like a lamb led to slaughter she entered the house. Her mother wouldn't even look at me. She just slammed the front door.

My daughter had just re-entered hell.

My daughter had just re-entered hell.

A month later my phone rang.

I looked to see who was calling and suddenly a black cloud came over me.

It was my ex.

Why was she calling? I hated that woman.

All she said was that our daughter had run away again and that this time nobody knew where she was. Then she hung up.

I sat there stunned, staring at my phone.

So that was it. My poor daughter. She had run away for good and nobody, not even her friends, knew where she had gone.

I called everyone I could think of who knew her. In time I learned that she might be staying at a house in a city several hours away. With further research I got a sketchy address and I drove to that city's local police department. I informed them that my daughter, a minor child, had run away from home but we had an address where she might be staying.

The police went to the address but could not find her. Impressing upon the occupants the seriousness of their search they managed to get other names and addresses and went to those places informing everyone that if anything happened to this young girl, they could all be held responsible.

The next day the police called and told me that my daughter had walked into the police station and turned herself in. Apparently, threats of prosecution to those people had worked.

But when I arrived at the police station to pick her up, I found out she had been transferred to the State Suicide Prevention Center for troubled teens in another city.

The officer told me that because the mother had primary custody, he intended to release her to her mother, but that my daughter had adamantly refused. The officer said they didn't know what to do with her. They couldn't hold her as a delinquent as she hadn't broken any laws. So he told her that the only way for them not to release her to her mother was if she told them she was suicidal. If she was suicidal, they could send her to a locked-down institution for suicidal teens where she would at least be taken care of until things could be figured out. So she told them she was suicidal and that's why they transferred her there.

The officer said to me, "Mr. Partridge, may I strongly suggest you figure something out for your daughter because as it stands right now she absolutely will not go back to her mother's house."

My daughter wasn't suicidal and never has been. But she had bought herself some time.

---

*I found out she had been transferred to the
State Suicide Prevention Center.*

Now a temporary resident at the Suicide Prevention Center and shielded from any intimidation and threats from her mother and stepfather, my daughter found the strength to oppose her mother. She demanded to be released to me, which the counselors were agreeable to do.

According to my daughter, this sent her mother on a rampage. Recognizing the real possibility that she was going to lose custody of her daughter, she criticized and belittled me to the counselors and psychologists. Her mother could not stand the thought that she might come live with me. But my daughter remained adamant. She told the counselors that she absolutely refused to ever again live at her mother's house.

In the end the Suicide Prevention counselors ruled that my daughter would be released to me freely, without conditions. So that was it. Parent War Five was over. After all those painful years my daughter was finally coming home.

But who was actually coming to live in my home? We were to find out soon enough.

But who was actually coming to live in my home?
We were to find out soon enough.

My daughter's world at her mother's house had been one of anger, hostility, and constant criticism. Tensions and stress made up her daily life. Attendance at school was a joke and homework non-existent. Life for my daughter was days and nights out with friends. All her teenage life she was a night owl, staying up until two or three in the morning and not waking up until the afternoon. Self-discipline, self-control, and self-restraint were foreign concepts.

Life at our home was the exact opposite, revolving around school, homework, and family and friends. All our children did well academically and got along socially.

Enter my daughter. Our lives must have been incomprehensible to her. Looking back I'm surprised she lasted the two months.

It was too much for her. She couldn't manage normal life. She had been too damaged. Within her was a raging war that demanded complete autonomy.

Within weeks after moving in with us she was sneaking out of the house at night. Because she was now sixteen, I found her a part-time job but she soon quit. After getting into trouble at school she stopped attending. Finally she just stopped coming home. The only thing that worked for my daughter was to hang out with friends as troubled as she.

*Within weeks after moving in with us
she was sneaking out of the house at night.*

So, basically self-emancipated, my daughter managed to arrange for herself places to stay, attended various schools, and subsisted by working part-time jobs.

Contact with my daughter again became sporadic.

Could things get any worse? What happened next shocked everyone. This time, it involved my son.

PARENT WAR 6: THE WAR BROUGHT ON BY MY SON

I was upstairs in my home getting ready to drive my son back to his mom's house. He was thirteen years old, halfway through the eighth grade. His weekend visit with me was coming to an end, so I called downstairs to tell him to get into the car.

Instead, he came upstairs into my bedroom, sat down, and startled me by calmly telling me that he wasn't going home, that he wouldn't be living with his mother any longer, and that he was now going to live permanently with me.

I looked at him trying to absorb what he had just said. I asked him what he was talking about.

He again told me in a matter-of-fact voice that he was now at my house and wouldn't be living with his mother any longer.

He again told me in a matter-of-fact voice that
he was now at my house and wouldn't be
living with his mother any longer.

I asked him if his mother knew anything about this and he said she had no idea and that he would let me tell her.

I asked him why he wanted to leave his mom. My son told me that the problem wasn't his mom—that he didn't mind living with her at all. The problem, he said, was his stepfather. He couldn't go through another baseball season with this man. He was impossible to be around during Little League baseball. The stepfather constantly criticized and yelled at him before, during, and after games.

I already knew the stepfather was a zealous baseball fan and a self-appointed coach to my son. But I had no idea of the extreme criticism and yelling and intense pressure he had put on the young boy. My young son couldn't throw or hit a baseball without facing his stepdad's tirades on how badly he had played—and all this had gone on since he was seven years old.

My son told me that a few weeks ago his stepdad told him to get his mitt and go outside to play catch with him. Dutifully he got his mitt and ball and they began playing catch. Once again my son was forced to endure the barrage of anger and frustration of his stepfather for not throwing the ball perfectly. He could never throw it hard enough or accurately enough to please that man.

It was the last straw for my thirteen-year-old. He decided he was not going through another season with his stepdad and that when he came to my house for one of our weekends, he would never return to his mom's house again.

I could see this wasn't a knee-jerk reaction on his part, that he had spent a great deal of time thinking about when and how to make his move to my house.

But all this was news to me. I needed some time to think this through.

I tried to process how the move could happen. I told him that maybe I could talk to his mom and we could work something out, especially with his stepdad. Maybe we could get through this baseball season so that he could finish eighth grade down at his mom's house and then make the move up to my house to attend high school.

My son said emphatically, "Dad, you can't say one word to mom and then leave me down there. That would be impossible. Remember what happened to my sister."

I just stared at my son blankly. I asked him, "What do you mean? What happened to your sister?"

He looked at me and realized that I didn't know.

"You don't know, do you? You don't know what mom did to my sister. Remember the court battle you had with mom years ago over trying to get my sister to live with you? And that she wouldn't tell the court mediator what was really going on at our house? You don't know why she caved in and didn't say anything, do you?"

I said no.

"Once mom learned that she wanted to live with you and that you were going to go to court to get her, both mom and my stepdad put her through weeks of screaming and threats. I'm not kidding you, Dad. It was horrible. The first few days it was solid screaming, then after that total silence, a few days later threats by them to throw her out of the house for good, then another few days of putting on her all this guilt about how she let them down. By the time my sister talked to the court mediator, she was terrified of what they would do to her. So do you know what she said to the court mediator? She was so scared of mom that she even talked against you."

My son continued, "I saw what happened to my sister, how mom and my stepdad forced her to go back on everything she told you. I watched what they did to her and I knew that when the time came for me to live with you, I could never, ever tell them.

"Dad, that's why if I go back down there tonight you can't say anything to mom. If it came out I wanted to live with you, you don't know what they'd do to me. I couldn't take it."

"You don't know, do you? You don't know
what mom did to my sister."

I just sat there in shock.

I couldn't believe what I was hearing. I had just learned for the first time why, three years earlier, my daughter had backed off and said virtually nothing to the court mediator. Her mother and stepfather had ganged up on my then thirteen-year-old, harassing her and threatening her until she was forced to recant her story, crumbling before the court. My poor daughter was forced to bear alone this incredible emotional pressure, and I had been powerless to help. I never knew. From what my son was telling me, I couldn't believe that any parent could be so cruel and destructive toward her own children.

In a moment of anguish I asked myself, *What kind of animals were raising my kids?*

And here was my young son, figuring that the only way to rid himself of another grueling baseball season with his stepfather was to make the announcement at my home, where he could be protected from his mother's and stepfather's anger and wrath.

In a moment of anguish I asked myself, What kind of animals were raising my kids?

My son said that since he is now living with me he would leave it to me to call his mother and tell her the news.

I told him that the phone call would not go so well.

I told him his mother would go absolutely crazy and come at me with every lawyer she could find. I had lost every custody battle we ever had and was certain to lose this one, too. I told him that his sister had never recovered from that terrible court battle and that I didn't want the same thing to happen to him. I promised him I wouldn't breathe a word of our conversation to his mother. I appealed again to my son that maybe I could talk to his stepfather and try to work something out with him. But now it was getting late and he needed to get into the car.

He said to me that he wouldn't get in the car—that he wasn't going back.

I told him that he had to go back.

I told him to get into the car or else I'd carry him into the car. Either way, I said, he was going down to his mom's house. He said to me that yes, I could make him get into the car but when he got to his mother's house, in the middle of the night he'd sneak out and walk the forty miles back to my house. He asked me if I wanted him hiking all night, especially through some of the cities he'd have to go through to get to my home?

I said no.

He said if he was picked up and forced to return to his mom's house he'd just run away again the next night—would I want that?

"What about the court?" I asked him. "What are you going to do about them telling you where you have to live?"

But with a wave of his hand he dismissed any discussion about the court. He said the mediators or judges could make all the decisions they wanted about where he was going to live, but where were they in the middle of the night? At midnight he'd sneak out and walk the forty miles to my house.

He repeated that there was no way he was going through another baseball season with his out-of-control stepfather. He said he was going to live with me and that there was nothing anyone could do about it.

I lamented that a phone call to his mother would precipitate a full-scale nuclear war.

But he just shrugged his shoulders. He couldn't care less. Dealing with his mom and the mediators and the court was my problem. As far as he was concerned, he was now living permanently at my house and would leave the details to me.

So we sat there staring at each other. Neither of us said a word.

All my son could think about was the relief of never having to play baseball around his stepdad again.

All I could think about was the upcoming Nuclear Parent War.

I lamented that a phone call to his mother would precipitate a full-scale nuclear war.

I shuddered at the thought of the incredible hardship we were all about to endure, only to certainly lose again. And the expense. I could see myself spending several thousand dollars, with the likely prospect of the vicious battle destroying my son. As I looked into my son's eyes I could see that he was a very, very determined young man. But would he be able to sustain his decision after what we were about to go through?

I was stuck. Once again I would be relying on the words and promises of a minor child—this time my son, who was only thirteen years old.

After a long period of silence with us just sitting there looking at each other finally I said okay, I'd make the phone call.

This was going to be the phone call of the century, with my son's emotional health completely on the line.

As I picked up the phone, I knew I was about to unleash a full-scale nuclear war with no prisoners.

And the phone call proved to be everything I imagined—only worse.

Once his mother learned what the call was about, nobody would believe the hatred and venom that poured into the phone. What she said should never be said, not even to one's worst enemy. Saying she loathed me, despised me, and absolutely hated me would be mild terms for what I had to listen to. She was literally screaming at me. Her words and the volume of her words could not describe her bitter hatred toward me. She was convinced that I was pure evil. In her mind I had put our son up to this, that I had brainwashed him, and that he was just a pawn in my lifelong plan to remove him from her custody.

Once his mother learned what the call was about, nobody would believe the hatred and venom that poured into the phone.

Would she be receptive to hearing anything about our son's difficulties with his stepfather, about the daily barrage of criticism that was injuring our son emotionally? Not in the slightest. She accused me of coercing my son, swaying his young mind, and forcing him against his will to remain at my house.

She said in the clearest terms possible that if her son wasn't home by the scheduled time, she would have me thrown in jail. And she was not kidding. I told her he had refused to get into the car, and she all but spit at me over the phone. She mocked me. She knew I was quite capable of getting my son into the car and this proved to her that it was me, not my son, who was separating him from her. It was either obey the court or she would personally see me in jail.

She told me I had pulled this stunt with my daughter and was now doing the same thing with my son. She reminded me that I lost in court and would lose again. Only this time, she told me, she would see to it that I never saw him again, that if I didn't return my son immediately, she would not stop until all visitation privileges were removed and she had permanent custody.

She then demanded that I put my son on the phone. She wanted to hear this so-called decision of his in his own words. Reluctantly I called my son up to my room to speak to his mother.

The phone call lasted less than a minute as my young thirteen-year-old told his mother, in halting words, that he was going to stay with me and couldn't live with her any longer. Then he became very quiet as he listened to her. I watched helplessly as he nearly folded in half physically. He was bent over crying, overcome with emotion. I was convinced she was destroying our son with her venomous words. I lunged forward and grabbed the phone. I was shocked beyond belief at the force her words had on my precious son. I privately swore to myself that as long as my son was in my home, he would never speak to his mother again. She had lost all rights to this boy.

Back on the phone she told me one last time that she would see her son within an hour or else I would go to jail.

I ignored her threats. In fact, my son remained at my house that entire next week. It was that following Saturday morning I was served with a restraining order demanding that if I didn't return him immediately, I would be arrested and charged with child abduction and contempt of court.

I knew what she wanted. I was certain that she wanted her son back so that she could subject him to her dominance and pressure. She had forced our daughter to back down and was confident, I believed, that she could do the same with him. It must have infuriated her that my son was with me, making her powerless to bend his will to hers. With the restraining order I believed she was assured she would get her son back that day.

I suspected my ex and her attorney intentionally served the restraining order on Saturday morning, knowing that I had no way to retain an attorney. Meanwhile I could be arrested that very day.

I knew what we had to do. For the emotional safety of my son, we ran.

I knew what we had to do.
For the emotional safety of my son, we ran.

I threw some clothes into the Jeep and told my son to get his stuff together—we were going for a drive. I asked him not to ask me any questions—that we were going to take some time off and spend the next few days together.

So we left town. Nobody knew where we were, not even my wife. It was Super Bowl weekend and my son and I watched the game with a couple of hundred other people in the huge lobby of some hotel in some remote town. That Monday my wife took off from work and retained an attorney. She told the attorney the entire story of my son—about his stepfather and mother, what they had done to my daughter, and what they would do to my son if he went back to live with them. Believing every word my wife said and believing that my son's safety was on the line, this attorney immediately countered my ex's restraining order with one of his own, demanding that my son be allowed to stay with me until emergency court mediation— to which the judge agreed.

So with great relief my son and I were able to come home.

But I was already anticipating what would happen in emergency court mediation two days later.

From past experience I knew that mediation was going to completely favor my ex and go one hundred percent against me. But what else could I do? Here I was again, totally reliant on a child to do his part and say what he had to say. I knew that what I had to say would be considered meaningless by the mediator and by the judge.

So when the court date arrived, my son and I walked into the mouth of the beast.

My wife and her son, Matt, my son's older stepbrother, came along for moral support.

So when the court date arrived, my son and I walked into the mouth of the beast.

I could have written the script.

Just like every other court mediator, this one spent almost all of her time with my ex and her attorney, less time with my son, and virtually no time at all with my attorney and me. We barely sat down when the interview was over. It was also no surprise when the mediator recommended that my son be returned immediately to his mother's home. The court's overall rationale was that no thirteen-year-old should be allowed to bully the court into determining where he was going to live. And that's basically what my son was doing.

The irony of the situation was that, apart from my son's desperate situation, I actually agreed with the rationale of the court.

It was also clear to me that the mediator firmly believed that my son had been coached by me in his opposition to his stepfather and that I had maliciously influenced him against his mother. Again, the mediator resolutely determined that I was the trouble-maker, forcing my son to live with me out of vengeance against his mother.

After the mediator issued her terse recommendation favoring my ex, we all went before a family court judge for final determination. I sat with my attorney on one side of the courtroom while my son's mother and her attorney sat on the other side. My son, his stepbrother Matt, and my wife remained downstairs in the court holding room. On the stand the court mediator vehemently objected to the lack of due process and the clear fact that both the mother and the court were being bullied by me and my young son. She repeated that my son should be returned to his mother immediately.

The judge then turned to me and asked me if I had any objection to the mediator's recommendation. I told the judge that because of problems down at his mother's house my son refused to live with her any longer. I told him that if my son was forced to go to his mother's house, he had told me he would sneak out in the middle of the night and hike the forty miles to my house and that I did not want that to happen.

She mocked me by telling the judge that all the so-called problems at her home were simply fabrications of my imagination.

The judge then listened to my son's mother bitterly accuse me of brainwashing my son and of the way I grossly undermined her authority. She mocked me by telling the judge that all the so-called problems at her home were simply fabrications of my imagination. She then emphatically reminded the court of our past court cases and the fact that I was the one who constantly lost. The judge then turned his attention directly toward me, imploring me to allow my son to go back to his mother's house. He asked me why everything had to be so sudden? Why did my son suddenly have to make the move in the middle of a school year? Why couldn't he finish out the year at his mom's house? Why couldn't we go through the standard legal process? And why couldn't my son make the move to my house over the summer months?

The judge, fully agreeing with the court mediator and the mother, was clearly displeased with me. To move my son in haste would be, in the judge's viewpoint, disruptive to his schooling and home life.

What more could I say? I had already told the mediator and the judge that my son was having severe difficulties with his stepfather and, if forced to remain with his mother, he would run away. Would the judge believe me if I told him I was sure that if my son went back to his mother's house, his mother would try to destroy him the way she had my daughter? His mother would laugh off my 'imaginations,' deny any wrongdoing, and point out that I was already a documented troublemaker.

I had already told the mediator and the judge that my son was having severe difficulties with his stepfather and, if forced to remain with his mother, he would run away.

By this time I was pretty disgusted with the mediator and the judge. It was clear that nothing I could say was going to alter the direction the court was taking.

All I could do was trust that my son had the fortitude to drive the issue. I had done what I could for him and, as expected, failed. My son started this litigation and now he would have to see it to its conclusion. Everything now fell on him.

Judgment came down strongly against me. The boy was to be immediately returned to his mother. Of course, I wasn't surprised. My ex sat there glaring at me, hating me, hating everything about me. I knew she wasn't going to let this go. I knew there would be future battles for change in custody with me having as little time with my son as possible. I had begun this legal battle and she was going to finish it.

Judgment came down strongly against me.

Two sheriff's deputies came into the courtroom to wait for orders to escort my son from the waiting room downstairs to his mother's car. The judge turned to me as he was about to leave the courtroom and once again implored me to let the boy go back to his mother's home. I shrugged my shoulders and told the judge that I wouldn't try to stop my son from going to his mother's house.

It was now after 5 P.M., and court was adjourned. The judge rose and left the courtroom through the door behind the bench.

So that was it.

Several minutes passed and we were all standing around in the courtroom signing some papers when suddenly the door behind the bench opened and the judge, astonishing us all, hurriedly buttoning his court robes, re-entered the courtroom. He asked if everyone was still present. As we were all there, including the two deputies, he finished buttoning his robe, took his seat, and brought the court back in session. He then looked at me and asked if I had any objection to my son living with his mother. I told him my son had some serious objections. But I would ask him again to go back to his mother's house.

The judge, with honest emotion, implored me to let the boy return to his mother's home. He then again adjourned the court and left.

I felt sick to my stomach in anticipation of what my young son was about to endure that evening. Once alone with his mother and stepfather, empowered by this latest court victory, I knew they would tear into him that night with a vengeance, decimating him emotionally, just as they had done to my daughter.

The time was now about 5:30 P.M., and it was dark outside. We were all still in the courtroom waiting on paper work when again the judge burst through the door, again hastily buttoning his robe, again surprising us all. We all just stood there without a sound and watched. The judge ascertained that everyone was still in the court room, asked everyone to be seated, and once again formally opened the proceedings. My attorney and I looked at each other bewildered at the actions of the judge. Had anyone ever seen this type of behavior before?

The judge looked directly at me and asked, "Where's the boy?"

The judge looked directly at me and asked, "Where's the boy?"

I told him that my son was in the special waiting room downstairs, and the judge ordered one of the deputies to go get him. We all sat there, including the judge, for several long minutes, in dead silence, as we waited for my son to be escorted into the courtroom. Within a few minutes the large doors opened and he appeared with the sheriff. The judge asked him to approach the bench. The deputy remained by the door while my son walked down the long aisle to stand before the towering judgment seat.

All eyes were on my son, so young and so all alone.

The judge asked him to come up the side steps and stand next to him. My son walked up and stood beside the judge. Then the judge stood and the two of them disappeared through the back door. It was quite a sight to see this huge six-foot eight-inch judge, his height exaggerated by his long robe, towering over my son as they left the courtroom. Nobody moved a muscle or said a word. We all sat stunned and silent. After several long minutes the door opened and out they came.

With my son standing beside him, the judge seated himself and gave this order. He said, "The boy is to go home tonight with his father. Both the mother and father, with their attorneys, are to appear before me in my chambers at 10 A.M. tomorrow." Down went the gavel.

With that he left the bench and didn't return.

My attorney just sat there for a long time and didn't move. He finally said that he had been practicing family court law for two decades and had never seen what had just happened. After a stinging rebuke from the court mediator against my son and me, after caustic remarks by my ex, after judgment had been issued from the bench against me—twice—the judge had reappeared a third time to speak with my son privately, then reversed his order, ignoring the mediator's recommendations, ruling that my son was to go home that night with me. My attorney was absolutely mystified.

My attorney was absolutely mystified.

Later in the car, I couldn't believe that my son and I were going home together. My son, my precious son. He, of course, seemed indifferent to the whole thing. I didn't question him that night about his conversation with the judge. The only thing he said was that he thought the judge was pretty cool.

The following day, with my son and Matt and my wife once again waiting downstairs in the court holding room, the mother and I and our attorneys went into the judge's chambers. Sitting behind his large desk he told us that in his eight years on the bench he had interviewed only two kids, my son being one of them. He said he was deeply impressed with my son. Usually people, particularly children, were intimidated by his huge size, but this young boy stood before him without fear, looking directly into his eyes, and calmly answered all the questions put before him. He was amazed and very pleased with the way my son handled himself. In the end the judge told us that he was going to do something very unorthodox. His ruling was that my son was to live with me. He knew that this was sudden and not the usual practice, but in his opinion it was the best solution.

I sat there as if in a dream. My son, my dear son, was finally coming to live with me. After all these years he was finally leaving that household that was filled with anger and criticism and hostility.

But what happened next completely shocked everyone, especially my attorney. The judge ordered that not only was my son to live with me but that any visitation schedule with his mother would be put into the young boy's own hands—*the hands of a thirteen-year-old*. My boy alone was to determine visitation with his mother. A special counselor would be appointed to meet with him to make the necessary arrangements.

With this judgment we left the courthouse. My attorney couldn't believe it. He told me that he had never seen control of visitation given over to a minor child.

So, Parent War 6 was over. My son finally came home.

Under the circumstances we were not anxious for him to see his mother. The special counselor simply told us to get in touch with him when we were ready to set up visitation. But no phone call was ever made. Nor did we try to contact his mother. And she never called us. As far as I was concerned it would be fine if we never saw that woman again.

As far as I was concerned it would be fine
if we never saw that woman again.

And I made good on my word. With my daughter out on her own and my son now living with me, we ceased all contact with that other household. Our association with her was finished.

THE MOM'S REVENGE

For the first time in over a decade, my ex-wife was completely out of my life. Nothing could have pleased me more.

Unlike my daughter who could not integrate into our family because of serious emotional damage, my son integrated quite well. He quickly settled into our family and school, made great friends, and excelled both academically and in sports.

I saw my daughter sporadically, and when we did get together my heart broke for her. Out on her own she was grossly ill-equipped to face the requirements of adulthood. She survived on part-time jobs, remained uninterested in learning a trade, and barely scraped by. Her life was spent hanging out with friends. Our relationship was fairly good, but her relationship with her mother was tumultuous, on again/off again. And, she had nothing to do with her stepdad.

Even though I was pleased beyond words to have my ex out of our lives, I was incensed by what I saw as her complete lack of sensitivity toward our son. In all the ensuing years that he lived with me, she rarely called him or tried to see him. I couldn't imagine a parent just cutting off one of her children. She knew about his success in academics and sports because my daughter would inform her. And even the rare times my son would see his mother (maybe a couple of times a year) she never asked about any of his interests or accomplishments.

Don't get me wrong. I loved the fact that we had practically zero contact with this woman. But I also felt for my son. I knew he felt abandoned by his own mother and that when they did see each other she didn't treat him very well.

Once when I was speaking with my daughter about her brother's and mother's rocky relationship my daughter agreed with me, then added in an off-handed way, assuming I knew what she was talking about, "Yeah, like that one Christmas at Grandma's. That was the worst."

"What Christmas?" I asked her. "What are you talking about?"

My daughter said, "You know, that Christmas day at Grandma's."

"No, I don't. What Christmas day?"

In disbelief, she replied, "You never heard about that Christmas? Oh my gosh, Dad. It was terrible. It was one of the worst days ever."

---

*"You never heard about that Christmas? Oh my gosh, Dad.
It was terrible. It was one of the worst days ever."*

She said, "Remember a couple of years ago how I managed to get my brother to go with me to Grandma's house for Christmas? Everyone was there—all our relatives—Mom, our stepdad, their two kids, my brother, me, all our aunts and uncles and their kids—a whole ton of people. And my Grandma's living room was literally filled with presents. I've never seen so many gifts before.

"Well, that Christmas morning we began handing out gifts. And everyone was getting all these gifts, and I mean lots of gifts. Everyone except my brother. I couldn't believe even the amount of presents I got. I had just moved into an apartment so I was getting a bunch of new appliances and dishes. Everyone got piles of gifts but there was my brother sitting there with nothing. Oh, he finally got one gift, a small box of See's candy. Can you believe it? He was sitting there with everyone laughing and handing out expensive gifts to each other.

"Everyone knew he was coming for Christmas and they all had plenty of time to get him something. But Dad, they intentionally ignored him. They were punishing him because they all knew he had chosen to live with you. I'm telling you, it was the meanest thing I have ever seen. I hated that day. I was so mad at my mom. I just died watching my brother sit there in silence."

Tears were welling up in my daughter's eyes. "You didn't know this, Dad? He never told you?"

"He never said a word."

I sat there staring at my daughter. I felt like a hundred pounds had just landed on my heart. My poor son. In despair I asked myself, *What kind of monsters are they?*" His own mother rarely sees him and when she finally does, she treats him like that?

This story confirmed to me that every negative thought I ever had about this woman was true. In my thinking every bit of enmity I'd ever felt toward her was completely justified. I believed their mother was the worst person in the world and again she proved me right.

And my children would have to continue to deal with this woman as their mother.

This story confirmed to me that every negative thought I ever had about this woman was true.

PART 2

TRANSITION

The introduction of some life-changing,
revolutionary Principles and Steps that will alter the
ways to deal with an ex—resulting in incredible
emotional health for kids

WHO COULD HAVE IMAGINED...

Following our separation my ex and I had waged six costly Parent Wars as well as individual conflicts so numerous they couldn't be counted. I hated the ground she walked on. I detested the air she breathed. I couldn't stand being in the same room with her.

Yet, everything their mother and I did to each other seemed to land directly on our kids—particularly our daughter, who took the full brunt of our Wars.

Yet, everything their mother and I did to each other seemed to land directly on our kids—particularly our daughter...

My daughter was now completely lost—a once vibrant young girl now a human shell—distraught, filled with rebellion, unskilled, unprepared, and unable to manage an adult world or normal adult pressures and responsibilities.

Who could ever imagine that she would experience such an amazing turnaround?

Over the next ten years she would go from hating herself to loving her life; from hurting herself to honoring her body; from incorrigible and damaging behavior to responsible behavior; from someone who couldn't write a complete sentence to a senior in college and soon to graduate; from someone whose friends were as damaged as herself to a successful marriage and children; from living off of friends to owning her own beautiful home; from someone who could not hold down a part-time job to rising to an executive level within a national company.

What happened to my daughter was nothing short of miraculous. What I had discovered worked!

QUESTIONS THAT WOULDN'T GO AWAY

Once I became a separated parent myself, I became aware of a huge number of separated parents who, like me, lived with endless complaints about their exes and problems with their kids.

Some of what I saw made sense: troubled parents producing troubled kids, good parents producing good kids.

But I also saw things that didn't make any sense. Sometimes really good separated parents—responsible separated parents— had deeply troubled children.

I would wonder how such great parents could have such damaged kids.

I would wonder how such great parents could have such damaged kids.

This curiosity led me to my present career—working with separated parents.

Over the next fifteen years I spoke personally with thousands of separated parents, gathering reams of stories and information, observing countless failures and successes. And over this decade and a half, clear patterns began to emerge.

THE STRUCTURES WITHIN

Working exclusively with separated parents was like having a front row seat watching the effects of the staggering loss and heartbreak on parents and their kids.

I saw the incredible influence of parents' behavior on their children.

I saw how the words and actions of parents—or their lack of words or actions—penetrated the hearts of their children, deeply affecting and altering them.

And I saw the effects of parent behavior linger throughout the children's lives.

And I saw the effects of parent behavior
linger throughout the children's lives.

I have met with innumerable adults well into their forties and fifties who continue to be affected by a parent's rejection or some gross irresponsibility that occurred decades ago. And when they talk about it, all the emotions surface like it happened yesterday.

Why the lifelong effects? Why do parents have such long-range influence on their children?

The reason is because of their biological connections. Through the evidence of DNA, children are biologically made up of half their mother and half their father.

Using the structure of a building to represent the child's internal framework, we see the half mother and half father.

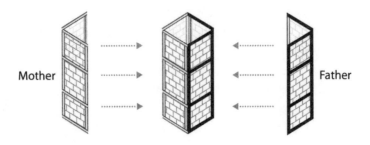

Illustration 1: Children have an internal framework
made up of half mother and half father

But the connections are far more than just physical. The biology shared between parents and their children appears to also include parts of the parents' emotional, mental, social, and perhaps even their spiritual makeup.

Coaches, teachers, stepparents, and non-biological guardians may be influential in the lives of children, but the biological parents can never be discounted. Non-biological adults *may* indeed influence the kids but the children's biological parents have impacted and will impact them deeply—even parents who are distant or are no longer part of a child's life.

One fellow told me that a particular coach over a period of eight years had far more influence on him than his grossly irresponsible parents, an influence that was life-altering for him.

I agreed with the fellow, but he shouldn't so quickly discount his parents. Where did he get his natural ability to play sports in the first place? And, where did he get his intense attention to detail and his natural leadership ability? If he thinks it all came from his coach, he needs to think again.

Whether living or not, present or absent, parents will always play a strong role in their children's lives.

It's the biological connections between parents and their children that give the parents their awesome—and at the same time potentially destructive—*access* directly into the hearts of their kids.

---

*It's the biological connections between parents and their children that give the parents their awesome—and at the same time potentially destructive—*access *directly into the hearts of their kids.*

Consider what happens when a child is negatively impacted by the ongoing actions of an irresponsible mother. As represented in Illustration 2, this mother's choices have caused significant emotional damage to the mother side of her child's internal framework.

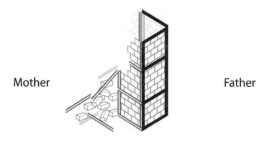

Illustration 2: The damaged mother side of the child

If this mother had been a responsible parent, her child would have remained structurally whole. But the years of neglect and poor behavior by the mother caused her child severe emotional damage.

Again, using a building to illustrate a child's internal framework, Illustration 3 shows the effects on a child negatively impacted by the ongoing actions of his irresponsible father, causing damage to the father side of the child:

Mother   Father

Illustration 3: The damaged father side of the child

The father, having no idea that his child is made up of half of him, is oblivious to the deep connection between himself and his child. Nor does this father have any clue as to the incredible impact of his self-centered and careless activities on his child, causing the child immense internal destruction.

Below is a child's internal framework when both parents live grossly irresponsible lives. The entire framework has been damaged.

Mother  Father

Illustration 4: The damaged mother and father sides of the child

If not repaired, any internal damage inflicted by a parent can last a lifetime.

One mom said to me, "Sure, my ex and I have made some mistakes, but kids are resilient."

But that's the problem. Broken kids are not resilient. Broken kids usually don't get over it.

Broken kids are not resilient.
Broken kids usually don't get over it.

MY DISCOVERY

So, who damages kids?

Bad parents damage their children.

Because of their biological connections—giving parents powerful access directly into the hearts of their kids—and because of their poor behaviors, bad parents break down their children's internal structures.

But bad parents are not the only ones who can damage their kids.

Good, innocent, faithful, responsible, wholesome parents can also damage their kids.

And, good kids can damage themselves.

I've seen good parents cause their children terrible structural damage. And, I've seen responsible children cause themselves severe damage while their parents have no idea that structural damage is even taking place.

How is this possible? How can good parents damage their children, and how can good kids damage themselves?

The answers are found in the following two Principles.

PRINCIPLE ONE

Principle One: What parents do to each other,
they do directly to their kids.

It is a pattern repeated endlessly: How parents respond *toward each other* directly impacts the emotional health of their children.

What we as parents do to each other penetrates right into our kids. Animosity and bitterness between parents become toxins that pierce the souls of their children.

If parents are negative toward each other, those same negative responses cause deep structural damage in their kids.

Look at these common phrases good, well-meaning parents, say:

"Your mother is nothing but a hardship to me. She's taking me to court again."

"Your father's late again."

"I can't afford a baseball mitt. Your father doesn't pay me enough money."

"Your mother's spending all the money I give her on herself."

"Your father only cares about his girlfriend."

Even without speaking a word, we can send strong negative messages to our kids. Through the rolling of our eyes, our sighs, and our body language we say:

"He's worthless."

"I can't stand her."

"He's so selfish and self-centered. He's only taking our kids to Disneyland because he wants to go himself."

"She's pure evil. Everything about her is wrong."

"He fails at everything."

"I wish she'd just fall off the face of the planet."

"I'll never forget the hurt he has caused all of us."

And then there is what we say to our friends and relatives about our exes. If you think your kids aren't listening or aren't aware, think again:

"He's just the sperm donor."

"She's just the egg donor."

"I wish she'd just leave. We'd all be a lot happier."

"He's always out with his girlfriend."

"We can see where her priorities lie."

"He might as well have abandoned his kids."

What takes place between parents *is replicated inside the children*.

When a parent is in conflict with the other parent, one 'parent half' within the child is in conflict with the other half. With the child experiencing internal structural wars, breakdown and damage are going to occur.

One woman approached me at a conference and began telling me the faults of her ex, with her elementary school daughter standing right beside her. As the mother noticed me looking at her child, she quickly said, "Oh, I never speak against my children's father. I'm just telling you what he did." This mom had no idea that her words were piercing right into the heart of her young child.

Silence can be just as damaging.

How do we normally respond when our kids are all excited about going to a theme park next week with their other parent? We probably say nothing. Or, if we do say something, it is short and rarely enthusiastic.

But, it's our silence, our lack of interest, our short answers and changing the subject that will penetrate right into our children's structure, cracking it up.

How natural it is to shut out the other parent, to point out the other parent's faults and failures. We say what we want, get it off our chest, and feel perfectly fine.

But our children are not fine. Instead of being sources of healing and comfort we damage them by our words and attitudes against their other parent.

But, it's our silence, our lack of interest, our short answers
and changing the subject that will penetrate right into
our children's structure, cracking it up.

And it's not just what we say or don't say. It's what we *do* as well.

One mom who needed to work late arranged to have her sister drop off her kids for their weekend with their father. But when the father heard that his ex wasn't driving the kids, he refused to see the sister, reminding her that the custody papers stated clearly that his ex was to drop off the kids. He told the mother that if she didn't comply, he'd sue her in court.

One dad was always late—sometimes hours late—when picking up or dropping off his kids, and he knew it caused problems for his ex. The mother's list of missed schedules and events was long and maddening because of the deliberately hurtful actions of this father. Yet, the father was personally thrilled knowing he was causing his ex all these difficulties. He wanted to disrupt her life as much as possible.

Another dad had a special family reunion coming up and asked for a couple of extra days with his son so the boy could spend time with his cousins and relatives. His ex refused. Her reasoning? The father refused to give her any of his time when she needed it so why should she give him any of hers? Serves him right.

And the list goes on and on....

Parents can cause all the hardships they want to other people and it probably won't affect the children. But cause hardship to the children's other parent, and it will emotionally damage the kids. Children are irreversibly bound to both parents. *What you do to your children's other parent, you do directly to your children*.

Troubled kids can even come out of
great *households and* great *remarriages*.

Troubled kids can even come out of *great* households and *great* remarriages.

I know two parents, once married, both now in second marriages and doing well. Both parents are responsible, live in nice homes, and are involved with their kids. Yet their kids are emotional wrecks.

What a surprise for these two parents to learn that the *foundations* of emotional health in children are not based on the two parents' own personal happiness, or their wonderful second marriages, or their great home environments, or even their great parenting skills.

It's Principle One: *What parents do to each other, they do directly to their kids.*

What a surprise for these two parents to learn that the foundations *of emotional health in children are not based on the two parents' own personal happiness...*

With a closer look we discover that the two parents are in constant conflict. They often speak against each other, desiring to turn their children's loyalties away from the other household—and by doing this they are ravishing their children's hearts.

In all other aspects both parents are great parents. They love their kids and are providing for them in the best way they know how.

But Principle One is emphatic. Positive response and positive interaction between parents is what builds emotional health in kids.

Frequently, it's not the evil, adulterous parent only but the good, innocent, faithful *parent who messes up the kids.*

Frequently, it's not the evil, adulterous parent only but the *good, innocent, faithful* parent who messes up the kids.

One woman left her husband and moved in with her boyfriend, taking her young children with her. She and her boyfriend married as soon as their divorces became final. This mother holds no ill-will toward her former husband and would like her kids to remain as close to their father as possible. She has asked her ex to put aside their differences so they can get along as friends. There is nothing that would please this mother more than if the father would welcome her and her new husband when they see each other at their children's numerous activities.

The father, however, will have none of it. To this faithful father, his ex-wife cannot betray him, tear out his heart, take his children, divide up their assets, and then ask for everyone to just be friends. No way is this man going to have anything to do with his treacherous ex-wife or her wife-stealing husband.

So, which parent is causing the most damage to the children?

What began as injury to the children because of the actions of the mother has sunk to a whole new level with the continued negative actions of the father. The mother caused a one-time train wreck in the lives of her kids by breaking up the family, but the father is continuing this train wreck every day. It is his continued negative response toward his ex that is damaging his children. Now it is the father's actions, not the actions of the mother, that are so harmful to the kids.

The mother caused a one-time train wreck in the lives of her kids by breaking up the family, but the father is continuing this train wreck every day.

Regardless of who caused the separation, regardless of the fault or innocence of either parent, if one parent continues to behave in a negative manner toward the other parent, it will be those negative words and attitudes and actions that will tragically impact their kids.

It's not about fairness. It's not about right or wrong. It is about how parents respond toward each other that determines the emotional health of their kids. It's about Principle One: *What parents do to each other they do directly to their kids.*

But isn't this father right to believe that it is his evil, immoral, unfaithful, self-centered, godless, irresponsible, loathsome ex-wife who messed up their children?

The reality is it's usually the innocent parent, the faithful parent, the responsible parent, the parent who stands for truth, the parent who loves the most, the parent who has sacrificed the most, who will likely cause the most *ongoing* damage to the children. Why? Because it is this parent who most likely won't let the violations of the past go.

Look at this father. He's the good guy with regard to his separation. But he's the one hanging onto the past—all the betrayals and deceit and suffering—and remaining negative toward the other parent.

But isn't this father right to believe that it is his evil, immoral, unfaithful, self-centered, godless, irresponsible, loathsome ex-wife who messed up their children?

Even *neutral* responses between parents are damaging.

There was one set of parents who, once separated, behaved as if the other parent never existed. Since their children were older the parents had nothing to do with each other. Yet, their children were surprisingly troubled.

What went wrong? Unknown to these parents, it was their ongoing wholesale neglect of each other and the complete absence of any positive interaction between them that damaged their kids.

How can parents with zero positive comments or actions toward each other raise positive children? Principle One says it can't happen. *What parents do to each other they do directly to their kids.* What goes on between parents is duplicated internally within their children's structures. In this case the neglect between the parents has created this same neglect between the mother half and father half within their children.

Response is everything! The foundations of emotional health in children are built on how biological parents respond and interact with each other.

How can parents with zero positive comments or actions toward each other raise positive children?

Look at how I responded to my children's mother.

Because I knew nothing about Principle One at the time, I thought I could treat my children's mother any way I wanted—harboring animosity or criticism toward her or completely ignoring her—without any negative consequences for my kids.

And when my children began behaving badly, I, of course, blamed their mom. In my mind it was clearly her betrayal and her self-centered actions that had caused my children such distress. I, of course, was completely pure in my own eyes. Yet, by my treating my children's mother like dirt, I treated my children like dirt. By criticizing their mother I criticized part of them. By hating their mother I hated part of them. By ignoring their mother I ignored part of them.

By my treating my children's mother like dirt,
I treated my children like dirt.

I had no idea what I was doing. I had no idea that everything to do with stability and happiness for my kids rode on how I treated their mother.

One fellow, very concerned for his children, lamented that Principle One was virtually impossible for him to fulfill. He said that he has tried to build a good working relationship with his ex but his ex refuses to even acknowledge his existence.

But Principle One isn't about relationships.

Principle One is only about response.

Relationships are up and down and come and go. But it's the steady, consistent, and on-going positive responses by one determined parent that will start to build emotionally healthy kids.

I asked the man to be encouraged. He can begin. His good responses alone will go far in helping to restore his children to emotional health regardless of how his ex might respond in return.

This is the power and incredible influence of Principle One: *What parents do to each other they do directly to their kids.*

PRINCIPLE TWO

*Principle Two: What children do to their parents,
they do directly to themselves.*

The response of children toward their parents *impacts the children.*

How children react to their parents *determines their own emotional well-being.*

It's a mirror effect. Children become how they respond toward either parent.

If a child is at peace with a parent, peace will reflect back inside the child. If a child is rude and belligerent toward a parent, that same rudeness and belligerence will reflect deeply into the parent half of that child.

Response for response, attitude for attitude, children *become* how they respond toward either parent.

---

*It's a mirror effect. Children become how
they respond toward either parent.*

One mother left her husband and daughter to go live with another man. Devastated, the teenage daughter criticized her mother and withdrew from her. The father supported his daughter's behavior agreeing with her that her mother had become a worthless parent.

But what the father and daughter did not know was that when the daughter opposed her mother she opposed half herself.

She had become her own worst enemy.

In criticizing her mother she unknowingly criticized herself. In being rude and angry toward her mother she became rude and angry toward herself. In withdrawing affection from her mother she withdrew affection from herself.

How could she not become damaged? It soon became evident that some emotional pieces were missing. Within a couple of years the daughter began moving from relationship to relationship. Of course, everyone blamed the terrible mom.

In being rude and angry toward her mother she became rude and angry toward herself.

When a child opposes a parent, it's the child who suffers.

Sure, this mom was affected by her daughter's emotional withdrawal. But it was the daughter who became altered. *What the daughter did to her mother she did directly to herself.*

So, with the assistance of her well-meaning father, this daughter caused her own structural breakdown.

And it can get worse.

One mom, having been betrayed by her husband, objected to the way her sons innocently loved and accepted their father. She determined that her two boys would know the truth about their father and that his cheating and irresponsible behavior would never be honored or rewarded. Over time the mom was successful at turning the affections of her two kids away from their father.

Normally this mother would have influenced her children to never see their father again except that, in their case, their father had money. In the mom's eyes he could at least be useful. So she taught her sons that their father owed them for all the problems they were experiencing and that he should pay. She taught them well. They learned to extort money from their father, favoring him if he gave it to them, turning away from him if he refused.

How could the two sons not become emotionally damaged? *What they did to their father they did directly to themselves.*

Today the two sons, both professionals in the eyes of the world, are wrecks in their personal lives. Of course the mother and adult sons continue to blame the father.

> *Normally this mother would have influenced her children to never see their father again, except that the father had money.*

Name a separated parent who doesn't applaud when their children oppose the other, offending parent. Don't we endorse, to some degree, our children's disrespect toward the other parent? And aren't we pleased when our children finally recognize the other parent's true colors? Don't we want our children to avoid wrong behavior? Don't we want them to honor right choices and turn away from people who do wrong? Don't we want them to side with the truth?

So, why shouldn't we coach our children against their offending parent?

Because the results will be incredibly damaging to the children.

Don't we endorse, to some degree, our children's disrespect toward the other parent?

My son and daughter were two and five years old when their mother left, too young to develop negative opinions about her. So, I took on the task of training them against her.

I believed that if they accepted their mother, it meant that they would turn out to be like her—which would be an outrage to me.

So I taught them to oppose her. I told them that mommy should be home with us, that it was wrong for her to have left us. It was wrong for their mother to date other men, that she should only be with me.

I was convinced that I was teaching them the right things.

Soon my children began to clash with their mother. At an early age they would tell her about her wrongs. Of course, their mother hotly defended her actions, contradicting everything I said about her, countering with lists of my faults and failures.

She told them that she had hated to leave but she had to because of how I treated her. She explained to them that the only way she could ever be happy again was to leave the marriage.

When back with me my kids poured out everything their mother told them. "What?" I would say. "She said that? That's a bold-faced lie." Then I would lay out my defense and offer further criticisms of her. So back and forth it would go, our verbal wars dragging our poor little children deep into our animosities and conflicts.

When back with me my kids poured out
everything their mother told them.
"What?" I would say. "She said that? That's a bold-faced lie."

Here were my innocent children, loving me, vulnerable and open to me, looking to me, trusting in everything I had to say, and here I was pouring into their souls toxic information. Of course they would nod their heads in agreement. Of course they would fully support everything I told them. And then they would give their mother the same support and agreement. They were little children—what else could they do? The results were confusing and structurally devastating to them.

And of course when they were older they would make up their own minds as to who was right and who was wrong, favoring one parent over the other—all to their terrible damage. Our lethal conflicts and accusations freely invaded their hearts—particularly my daughter, who took the full impact of our Wars.

What began as a nightmare between my ex-wife and me ended up with our kids carrying our nightmares deep within themselves.

What began as a nightmare between my ex-wife and me
ended up with our kids carrying our
nightmares deep within themselves.

This was Principle Two at work: *What children do to their parents they do directly to themselves.*

THE NEGATIVE ACTIONS OF THE MOM (PRINCIPLE ONE) AND THE NEGATIVE ACTIONS OF THE CHILDREN (PRINCIPLE TWO) BRING DOWN THE CHILDREN

A fellow in his mid-twenties called me to ask if I would be willing to speak to his organization. He told me he had heard me speak about the Two Principles before and that what I had to say applied directly to his family and might be of some help to members of the group.

I asked him to tell me about his family.

He said, "My four younger brothers and sisters are basically human wreckage."

His mother and father divorced when he was an infant, and his mother later remarried and had four children with her second husband. Eventually this husband left the mother for someone else, forcing the mom to raise her children by herself.

Over the years the mother had remained bitter against the dad. She recruited her children to join with her against their father, taking every opportunity to remind them of their father's failures.

I could hear the sadness in his voice as he described the emotional trauma this had on his brothers and sisters. And he could see how the wars of the mom against the dad attacked the father half of the kids (Principle One), and how the wars of the children against their own father became their wars against the father half of themselves (Principle Two).

Saying that his younger brothers and sisters were basically human wreckage was amazingly accurate.

Here's what they looked like inside:

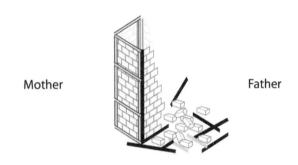

Mother   Father

Illustration 5: The completely damaged father part of the children

ARE PRINCIPLES ONE AND TWO THE ONLY PRINCIPLES THAT BUILD HEALTHY KIDS?

Of course not.

In buildings, it is the floors, walls, windows, and elevators that make the building usable. But these components can only be added once the structure of the building is up and intact.

It's the same way in children—essential components such as self-discipline, self-reliance, personal responsibility, virtue, patience, and self-control are what make kids successful, but they can only be added to an intact internal framework.

Crack a tall building's internal structure or remove its structural framework and all the essential components added to it, like floors, walls, and windows, become useless.

In the same way, crack the internal structure of a child and the essential components added to the child, like self-discipline and personal responsibility, won't work well either.

Stable structures in buildings and in kids support the essential components.

Preserve the children's internal structures—or restore them—and you can add all the components you want.

Consider my daughter.

Any attempt on my part or her mother's part to control our teenage daughter was completely futile.

Imagine me trying to talk to my daughter about how she styled her hair, or her choice of friends, or the importance of making good grades while inside her were all these raging wars and massive structural breakdown. It was impossible. She couldn't hear a word I was saying. Within her were these incredible struggles and ongoing personal failures and overwhelming guilt—and here I was talking to her about her hair?

Within her were these incredible struggles and ongoing
personal failures and overwhelming guilt—
and here I was talking to her about her hair?

Even when she tried to improve herself, she failed. Her dreams of living just a basic life were constantly sabotaged by her inability to function normally. Her conclusion: Why try?

Dominated by her internal brokenness all she was capable of doing was making poor decisions and displaying difficult behaviors.

What my daughter needed was not another lecture on personal improvement but major internal structural repair.

Years later, when I had developed the Two Principles, I finally had the tools to begin to rebuild her. I couldn't control my daughter's behavior, but I could rebuild her soul. And once I figured this out and began following the Principles, miraculous changes began to take place inside my daughter.

I couldn't control my daughter's behavior,
but I could rebuild her soul.

MY REACTIONS AGAINST MY OWN RESEARCH

When I first developed the Two Principles and began to understand them, I realized they were pointing fingers of blame directly at me. They accused *me* of damaging my own children.

The Principles were saying that yes, my ex's behaviors did indeed damage our children, *but I was responsible, too.*

That didn't sit well with me.

I immediately opposed my own findings.

How dare these Principles cast an accusing eye at me! How dare they suggest that my children's negative reactions against their mother were damaging to them!

Isn't it true that it's the inconsiderate, irresponsible, selfish, and self-centered parents—parents who abandon their children or who abuse them—who cause their kids to have problems?

And since this is true, I believed it was my ex's self-centered and negligent actions against my children that damaged them. She's the one the Principles should accuse of messing up my kids, not me.

But now here are the Two Principles telling me that I'm *also* responsible for my daughter's and son's structural damage.

No way. It can't be true.

My focus was on my ex's behavior. The Principles' focus was directly on me.

My focus was on my ex's behavior.
The Principles' focus was directly on me.

There was no argument on the part of the Principles that poor parent behavior damages kids. *Yes. Bad parents damage kids.* And they agreed with me that my ex was at fault. *Yes, my ex was at fault.*

But they also accused me.

Over time, as I continued working with hundreds of separated parents, I saw that the Principles were right, *that it's not about terrible parent behavior as much as it is about terrible parent responses*—that the real damage to children is caused by the hostile responses between parents and the hostile responses of kids toward their parents.

I ached to realize that for the past twenty years, all the responses my children ever heard from me about their mother were negative.

As I understood more about the Two Principles, I began to see that I was their chief offender.

My kids were in serious trouble and it was because of me.

I finally I got it.

What had I done to my kids?

In openly resisting their mother, in speaking against her, in disrespecting her, in loathing her, in hating the ground she walked on, I had inserted all of this animosity forcefully and directly into the hearts of my kids. It was *my* actions against my children's mother and *my* training my children to oppose their mother that had dismantled them.

It was sheer anguish for me to realize that all my children had ever known was their parents in conflict. For the past two decades my focus had been entirely against their mother. Growing up, my children had never experienced positive responses between their parents. From their childhood to adulthood their mother and I had always been in some sort of Parent War.

In every aspect and at every point the Principles opposed me.

They opposed what I believed, clashed with what I stood for, disagreed with how I reacted to my children's mother, and fought against how I taught my kids to disrespect her.

They forcefully stated to me that I had failed my children, that I wasn't the great parent I thought I was, and that I had brought to ruin the mother side of their internal structures.

It wasn't my daughter who had failed as a teenager. It was I who had failed as a parent. It wasn't my daughter's terrible choices. It was my terrible choices. It wasn't her bad behavior. It was my bad behavior.

It wasn't my daughter who had failed as a teenager.
It was I who had failed as a parent.

If it is true—and it is true—that *what parents do to each other deeply impacts the structural health of their children*, then I was surely to blame.

If it is true—and it is true—that *negative responses of children toward a parent impact their structural health*, then my turning my son's and my daughter's hearts against their mother most certainly caused them structural damage.

I could have probably prevented most of our Parent Wars.

I could have pursued resolutions other than hating her. I could have brought peace between us. It would have taken some time and effort but I could have established a working relationship between us. But no, I chose to oppose their mother. For years I wanted my children's mother out of my children's lives.

My poor children.

My daughter later told me that all she wanted in her life was to be normal, to be able to make normal life choices, and to be able to take control of her life.

My daughter later told me that all she wanted in her life was to be normal, to be able to make normal life choices, and to be able to take control of her life. But the brokenness and the internal battles raging inside her prevented her from moving in the direction of stability, normalcy, and peace.

It was time for me to stop blaming her mom.

To begin the process of restoration in my daughter, I needed to quit focusing on the behaviors of my ex. I needed to quit looking at her as the problem. I needed to begin looking at myself as the problem. I needed to change my own behaviors and pay attention to my own responses as a parent.

SOLUTIONS BECOME INCREASINGLY CLEAR

Once the Two Principles became clear, solutions for troubled, separated-parent families became easier to figure out.

One stepmom was about to separate from her stepfamily because the conflicts with her stepson appeared to be unsolvable. So she contacted me.

This stepmom told me that her sixteen-year-old stepson was a good kid, but not to her. Around her he was critical and insulting.

She demanded that her husband stand up to his son's rude behavior but the husband refused. In fact, the dad declared the stepmom to be the problem, blaming her for the boy's negative reactions. So the family was at an impasse. Having lost support from her husband, the only solution the stepmother could see was to leave the marriage.

As I interviewed her, I identified that in their case the problem wasn't between the stepmom and the stepson as everyone thought. The problem was between the dad and his ex-wife.

Following their separation things went well for the dad but not for his ex and she resents it. Blaming her ex for her difficulties, she has successfully influenced her son against his dad and stepmother. But because the boy is reluctant to outwardly oppose his father, he takes out his frustrations on his stepmom.

I told this couple that if the dad and his ex were at peace, the problem between the stepmom and her stepson would likely vanish.

...if the dad and his ex were at peace, the problem between the stepmom and her stepson would likely vanish.

And it did.

Both the father and the stepmom immediately agreed to give the mother her rightful place of respect as the boy's mother and ceased criticizing her. They began speaking well of the mom to the boy, complimenting her and telling respectful stories, funny stories about the mom, knowing these stories would be communicated back to her.

What was also extremely helpful was the stepmom taking the heroic measure of inviting the mom to coffee, which the mom accepted.

A few months later the stepmother reported that there was almost a miraculous change in her stepson's behavior. They are actually getting along. The dad even reported that his own relationship with his son is much better.

What was thought to be a stepmother/stepson problem was actually a Parent War problem. Once the exes experienced peace, their son also calmed down. This is Principle One: *What parents do to each other directly impacts their children.*

Even future behaviors became predictable.

I was visiting a stepfamily at their home when a large fully detailed pickup truck came roaring up the street, coming to a stop in front of the house. It was the boy's dad arriving to pick up his son for his weekend time. I happened to be standing outside when the truck pulled up and was glad to meet this man who was groomed and dressed as immaculately as his truck. I introduced myself and told the man I was visiting the mom and stepfather of his son. The father was cordial and talkative, and we had a nice few minutes together while waiting for his son to come outside.

But when his twelve-year-old appeared, the father became noticeably agitated. He roughly asked his son why he didn't have his extra jeans and shirts. When the boy gave him a blank stare, the father began pouring out his frustrations on the boy. "Can you believe your mother? She said she'd have your clothes ready when I picked you up and they're not. Figures. She forgot. Can't your mother do anything right? Has she ever done anything she says she will do? Not on your life. You go back into that house and get those clothes!"

Can't your mother do anything right? Has she ever done anything she says she will do? Not on your life.

Once the son went back into the house, some time passed before we saw him again. I later learned that the mom and son spent some frantic minutes trying to locate the clothes and finally gave up. They couldn't readily be found—probably being mixed in with his stepbrother's clothes. So, with his head lowered and shoulders sagging he came outside clearly dreading to inform his already stressed-out father that they couldn't find the clothes, but that they would be ready the next time he came. With the dad still fuming they both got into the truck and roared away. I felt sorry for the boy as I stood there watching the blur of steel and chrome disappear down the street, knowing that he was continuing to get an earful of his father's anger toward his mother.

So there it happened. Right in front of me the father verbally cut into the boy's heart. Without a clue as to the powerful access he has into his son's life, in speaking against the mother, he damaged the internal structure of his son. All the boy could do was accept the injury, hang his head, and feel bad. It only took a few choice sentences from this father to bring this happy and bright young boy down into emotional heaviness.

Because of the continued wars between the parents it wasn't difficult to guess this young man's future. Now in his twenties, the boy is a disappointment to both parents because of his obvious immaturity and irresponsibility. Of course, each parent blames the other parent.

Right in front of me the father verbally cut into his son's heart.

But, sometimes things just don't add up.

I was one of the speakers at a large two-day conference for single parents. We had been asked to arrive early and gather together to meet the keynote speaker. When introduced to us he told us his personal story—how his first wife left him and how he retained primary custody of his daughter.

He informed us about his second marriage and how pleased he was that his daughter had grown to care for her stepmother, even calling her Mom. In fact, he laughed as he told us that his daughter was now calling her bio-mother her 'egg donor,' saying things like, "I'm going over to the egg donor's house tomorrow."

In fact, he laughed as he told us that his daughter was now calling her bio-mother her 'egg donor,' saying things like, "I'm going over to the egg donor's house tomorrow."

He ended his introduction by telling us how great things were in his second marriage and how great his daughter was doing in their stepfamily.

At this point I was skeptical.

What he was saying about his daughter didn't add up.

How could his daughter be doing so well? She had to be adversely affected by her parents' ongoing wars. Principle One: *What parents do to each other, they do directly to their kids.*

And how could the daughter treat her mother so badly and not have damaged herself? Principle Two: *What children do to their parents, they do directly to themselves.*

Since the divorce occurred years earlier, she by now had to be negatively affected. But this speaker was describing something entirely different, saying everything about his daughter was fine.

After thinking about this speaker's story throughout the two-day conference I concluded that he had embellished his story. I believed that he got caught up in the emotions of the moment, telling us more about what he wished would happen with his daughter than how things really were.

I thought I would wait it out and see what I could learn.

It didn't take long.

Before the conference was over, the speaker pulled me aside and told me that his daughter was having some serious behavioral problems.

Now everything made sense.

I was sorry for the father and I sincerely wished things had been different for his daughter—but the rules are the rules.

...I sincerely wished things had been different for his daughter— but the rules are the rules.

OTHERS' REACTIONS TO THE TWO PRINCIPLES

Many separated parents have difficulty with the Two Principles when they first hear about them.

Not surprising. So did I.

Most of the opposition comes from people who believe they have been, and still are, the good parents.

Good parents object to any suggestion about giving honor or respect to the bad parent.

And they object, as I did, to any suggestion that they are responsible for any of their children's difficulties. They continue to insist, as I used to, that it's the irresponsible and destructive behaviors of the bad parent that have damaged their kids.

Good parents object to any suggestion about giving honor or respect to the bad parent.

During a single-parent/blending family conference a woman said to me, "I really like what you have to say—but it doesn't apply to me. My ex is the one who needs to hear this. He's the one who left me for another woman and the one who has hurt my children."

I said to her, "I was talking about your response toward your ex. How's that going?"

"Oh, I never speak against my ex. It's my ex who speaks against me."

"When was the last time you said something positive about the other parent to your kids? And what did you say?"

"No. You don't understand. Let me tell you what he's done to my kids and me and you'll see why he's the problem. He dated my best friend behind my back and then married her…He lied to me about working late…He stole all our money…He won't return any of my texts or calls…He's the one who is irresponsible…" and on and on.

I asked, "So how are your children with their father? Are they in touch with him and do they get along well with him?"

"Look. I wasn't the one who deserted my kids," she said. "He barely attends their practices and games…He was late to his own son's birthday party…It's clear to my kids he has chosen his new wife over them…He won't even call his children regularly. I don't blame my children for withdrawing from their father after being treated this way."

Parents seem to make it a challenge to prove to me why,
in their *case, the Two Principles don't apply to them.*

Parents seem to make it a challenge to prove to me why, in *their* case, the Two Principles don't apply to them. They bring up the most horrendous stories they can think of about their exes to prove to me their opposition is justified.

One parent confronted me saying, "My wife left me, took my kids, sued me in court and got my retirement and, according to you, I'm supposed to do what? Just act like nothing's happened? Easy for you to say…."

A woman asked, "He takes our eleven-year-old son to inappropriate movies. How can I be okay with that?"

Another said, "He drops our kids off at the Mall completely unsupervised while he takes off all day with his girlfriend. And you're asking me to put up with that type of behavior?"

One very defensive mom was so angry she could hardly speak to me. "My ex is a Disneyland dad. When the kids return home, it takes me three days to get them back to normal schedules and normal controls. He makes me look like the bad parent. And you're saying I'm supposed to just respect this guy? He's the one who should respect me."

And then a dad told me, "Every time my kids come back home, I hear about what their mother did on her weekends. 'Hey Dad, we stayed at Dan's house last weekend. He's really cool. He's got a swimming pool.' Or, 'We like Rob a lot. He made us banana splits.' Another time my kids said, 'We don't like Andy. He made mommy cry.' The dad asked, "And you're saying I'm just to accept all this?"

A woman asked, "He takes our eleven-year-old son to inappropriate movies. How can I be okay with that?"

The problem is parents are focused more on the behaviors of their ex than on what is required to build structural health in their kids. Because of the ex's terrible behaviors they act as if they are exempt from any responsibility to respond well. To them, the other parent has become irrelevant to their children's emotional health and stability.

But the Principles absolutely disagree. Children are still biologically connected to both parents. It is both parents who hold the keys to their children's well-being.

Positive response between parents is everything.

"THE GIFT OF MY DAD"

One man told me that when he was six years old, he remembered his mother crying all the time. He knew his father was with another woman and the cause of his mother's unhappiness. He determined then and there that he would no longer be friends with his dad. But this mother, after hearing her son say something disparaging about his father, told him in no uncertain terms that he was never to speak against his father again. She told him his father was a good man and loved him very much and that he was to love his father back.

And his mother made good on her words. This man said that he has never heard his mother speak a critical word about his father, and that she always encouraged him to spend as much time with his father as he wanted, even if it meant living with his dad—which he did for several years while growing up.

Then this man made a statement I'll never forget. He said to me, "When I was six years old, my mother gave me the gift of my dad."

This mother preserved the dad half of her son.

No wonder this young man grew up to be stable, responsible, and emotionally healthy.

It's stories like these that just don't stop. Over and over again the Two Principles continue to prove themselves as the solutions to building emotionally healthy kids.

THE SEVEN STEPS

So what do we do now? How do we fulfill the Two Principles? What does positive response toward our ex look like?

Are we supposed to become friends?

Are we to invite the ex and the ex's partner to a barbecue in our back yard?

How are we to communicate with the other parent? How supportive are we to be? Are the Two Principles suggesting that we just surrender to our exes and let them have their way? Are we to just say yes to everything?

Can't we oppose anything about our exes? Are we to just ignore the years of treachery against us and act as if nothing ever happened? What kind of standards will we be teaching our children? Can't we instill in our children right from wrong? What can we say and what should we not say? Is admitting to our kids we have done things wrong toward the other parent the best thing for them?

We now have the Two Principles, but how are we to fulfill them?

Are we supposed to become friends? Are we to invite the ex and the ex's partner to a barbecue in our back yard?

Over time I learned the answers to all of these questions.

Having seen just about every kind of positive and negative response between separated parents, I developed Seven Steps that are critical to fulfilling the Two Principles and restoring children to emotional health.

Here they are:

Step 1: Understanding

Step 2: Acceptance

Step 3: Amnesia

Step 4: Mercy

Step 5: Neutral—Damaging

Step 6: Benefiting

Step 7: The Cost of Doing Business

STEP 1: UNDERSTANDING

A mom and I were talking about her separation and I asked her the same questions I ask everyone: How are you and your ex getting along and how are the kids?

Her response I've heard a thousand times.

"Their father is so incredibly self-centered. He acts purely out of his own interests and couldn't care less about the interests of his kids."

I asked, "How often do the children see their dad?"

"Let me tell you how bad this man is…" says the mom. And again I sat through a long detailed list of the other parent's failures and deficiencies.

"How are the kids?"

She said, "Fine." Then, without even stopping for a breath, she launched off on how selfish and irresponsible the father is and how he has failed his children.

There was no point in asking any more questions. Her focus was entirely on the incompetencies of her ex.

How interesting. I'll bet there was a time this woman was this dad's best fan, fully convinced that he was critically important in the lives of their children.

But now, since their separation, look how her opinions have changed. The dad, because of his behaviors, is no longer important in her life and therefore, she thinks, no longer important to her children's emotional health.

It was this change in Understanding—*her reversal of opinion toward the father*—that began to damage her kids emotionally.

It was this change in Understanding—
her reversal of opinion toward the father—
that began to damage her kids emotionally.

Of course, the mother sees herself as innocent and blames the father for her children's behavioral problems.

But to bring stability back to her children, this mother needs to go back to her original Understanding of the importance of the father.

Understanding is to acknowledge that *both* biological parents are critical keys to the emotional health of their kids.

If parents lose this Understanding, if parents quit acknowledging the importance of the other parent in the lives of their children, if they treat their exes with contempt or indifference and train their children to do the same, their children will experience internal emotional breakdown.

Understanding will never prevent this mother from privately acknowledging her ex's weaknesses and failures or make her blind to the bad decisions her ex may make regarding their children. Quite the opposite. Knowing her ex's problems and shortcomings and making decisions based on this knowledge can provide the children with much-needed safeguards.

But this mother crossed the line when she allowed the failures of her ex to cause her to *redefine* the father's importance in her children's lives.

Understanding says yes to privately being aware of the other parent's problems and faults. Understanding says yes to setting up as many safeguards for the children as are needed.

But Understanding insists that both parents acknowledge each other as vital to their children's emotional health.

Regardless of a parent's hostility, irresponsible behaviors, and personal failures—even child abandonment—both biological parents continue to be critical keys to the stability of their children.

This mother can't control her ex's behaviors but she can control hers. She can begin to respond well toward her children's father and help her children do the same.

This mother can't control her ex's behaviors,
but she can control hers.

What about foster care? What about adoption? What about alternative means of conception where children may never know their biological parents? What about absent parents or deceased parents? How does all this work?

The importance of the biological parents continues.

Children will always be half their biological mother and half their biological father.

Physical contact between parents and children is *not* a requirement for children to remain emotionally healthy.

What is required though, is for the acting parent (or caretaker) and the children to continue to maintain some form of respect and positive regard toward the absent parent(s). A single mom whose ex has abandoned the family could say to her children, "Look, your father and I had some real difficulties, and now he's gone. I'm sorry things didn't work out. Your father is not in our lives and that's the way it is. Let's continue to hope for the best for him and that things are going well."

See the positive response by this mom? *What parents do to each other they do directly to their children.* Then, with the help of their mom, it is up to her children to carry some sort of positive regard toward the absent parent. This is Principle Two: *What children do to their parents they do directly to themselves.*

One middle-aged woman, well dressed, approached me after hearing me speak and told me that the Two Principles clearly explained much of her troubled past.

Because this woman's parents were in and out of jail and drug rehab centers, as a child she had been made a ward of the state and was raised in foster care homes. In one particular home her foster parents criticized and joked disrespectfully about her parents for many years and she would join in with their negative attitudes and comments. During this time she barely saw her parents, having no desire to visit them.

Yet, living in a stable foster home, she was confused as to why she had this raging war inside of her. All during her teenage years she was a nightmare to be around, hostile to everyone, and constantly in and out of trouble. She told me that it had taken her thirty years to finally calm down from her troubled childhood. And even today she recognizes she is still struggling with some emotional damage.

But the Two Principles explained so much. Those foster parents, not Understanding how to maintain internal health in children, unknowingly contributed to her internal damage. The caregivers thought they were doing the right thing by helping the girl recognize right from wrong. Yet, unknown to everyone, teaching the daughter to ridicule and disrespect both her parents caused the girl to ridicule and disrespect both halves of her internal structure. And that is what certainly contributed to the terrible emotional warfare deep inside her.

Teaching the daughter to ridicule both her parents caused the girl to ridicule both halves of her internal structure.

What if the parents are unknown?

Nothing changes.

I know a woman, adopted as an infant, who loves her non-biological mother and father with the same care and devotion she would if they were her own biological parents. This woman always knew that she was adopted and her parents coached her to carry a positive attitude toward her birth parents. She was told that her birth parents were very young, still in high school when she was born, and that they were good individuals. It had been a very difficult decision for them to give her up, but they wanted their child to have a better life than they could give her.

Everything about the attitudes of the adoptive parents and their adopted daughter toward the birth parents was good and positive. Is it any wonder that this woman is today emotionally healthy?

Make no mistake about it. Although the adoptive parents were huge keys to the stability and well-being of their daughter, it was the girl's internal framework that was also critical to her emotional health. There is no way the parents would have been so successful with their adopted daughter—no matter what their child-raising skills—if the daughter were broken internally. The girl is still half her birth mother and half her birth father. Strike against her internal structure through criticism—or silence—toward her birth parents and she would have been a nightmare for her adoptive parents. Because those parents modeled a positive respect toward the birth parents, the daughter has a positive respect for herself: *What she does to her birth parents she does directly to herself.* This set the stage for a great life for this family.

Strike against her internal structure through criticism— or silence—toward her birth parents and she would have been a nightmare for her adoptive parents.

A mom approached me saying that she had a fertilized egg implant and that she and her partner are now raising her two-year-old daughter. She asked how the Principles worked in her case.

I told her that, like with adoption, other alternative means of conception are treated much the same way.

Attaining emotional health in kids is getting as close to the Principles and Steps as possible. This means the only thing this mother and her partner can do is to connect with their daughter as if they are the biological parents, see to it that their daughter treats them as if they are her own biology, and help their daughter carry some form of positive regard toward her actual biological parents (such as: "I'll bet your donor parents were talented artists just like you!").

Even the death of an ex doesn't change how parents or children should respond.

At a meeting with a group of separated parents I mentioned to one of the divorced moms that her recently deceased ex still plays an important part in her children's lives. The mother corrected me, saying, "No, he's dead."

In protest I said to the group that children will always be half their father, making this deceased parent a key to the emotional health of his children. Yet, out of the corner of my eye, I saw the woman turn to her friend and say, "No, he's not. He's dead."

I hope this mom will reconsider. Without positive responses about their father, the father half of her children will be neglected.

This is Step 1: Understanding. Understanding is to acknowledge that children are half mother and half father. Therefore, both biological parents—living or deceased, in their children's lives or not—will always be keys to the emotional health of their children and must be given considerable respect.

STEP 2: ACCEPTANCE

One man I knew was emotionally distraught when his wife left him and their daughter to go live with her boyfriend across town. Both he and his daughter were heartbroken. But his ex hardly noticed or even cared as she was busy building a new life for herself. The daughter found her mother's departure particularly difficult because she realized that she was no longer a priority in her mom's life. So, with the support of her father, the daughter withdrew from her mother and the mother's boyfriend.

But Step 2, Acceptance, has some urgent advice for this father:

Your daughter has been structurally damaged by her mother. If your daughter isn't taught correctly, the damage caused by her mother's departure will pale in comparison to the damage your daughter will suffer because of your negative responses toward the mother.

Yes, you and your daughter need time to grieve and work through this difficult event. And yes, you both need time before you decide on new directions for your lives.

But you are *out of time* when it comes to responding to the mother.

You must act immediately. Right now you have the ability to either dramatically increase the damage in your daughter or reverse the damage and restore your daughter to stability and emotional health.

Restoration for you and your daughter will begin when *you* Accept what has taken place with your ex.

Acceptance means letting your ex go.

Acceptance means to leave her alone.

Acceptance means to quit thinking everything she does is evil.

It means for you to Accept the reality that your ex is no longer with you, that she has moved on with her life, that she is with another individual, and that your daughter is now going to be raised between two separate households. You must force yourself to make peace with this life and these realities.

You have to quit fighting your ex. You have to quit making problems and quit trying to punish her.

Acceptance means to allow your ex to make decisions for her own life without any criticism or involvement from you.

Acceptance means to recognize your ex's boyfriend. It's acknowledging that this individual exists and that he is now part of your ex's life and therefore part of your daughter's life.

Acceptance also requires that you accept all the family members of this man—to quit opposing these individuals.

Acceptance means to recognize your ex's boyfriend.
It's acknowledging that this individual exists and
that he is now part of your ex's life and therefore
part of your daughter's life.

Acceptance does not mean you have to agree with the lifestyle or behaviors of your ex or her new family or anyone else, but it does demand that you begin to respond positively toward them.

Can you change anything about what has happened? Can you bring your ex back? Can you alter in any way whom she dates or chooses to be with? Since the answers are probably no, then you are obligated to Accept your ex, her boyfriend, and the life she has chosen for herself.

The emotional well-being of your daughter is riding on whether or not you choose to Accept your ex.

Can you bring your ex back? Can you alter in any way whom she dates or chooses to be with?

Certainly there are things this father cannot Accept about his ex.

Acceptance is intolerant of any ex who threatens to harm, or has harmed, the parent or children.

If the ex is involved in addictions or criminal behavior, or if the ex is threatening or abusive, all contact between the offending ex and the parent and children must immediately cease until safeguards are in place.

Even between cooperative exes, if emotions get out of hand, if conversations become uncomfortable, Acceptance is all about setting boundaries, saying no, ending phone conversations, and lessening personal contact.

Acceptance is *not* being a doormat, and certainly *not* being agreeable to everything the ex wants.

Acceptance will never prevent any parent from seeking to modify custody arrangements or child support, or to defend themselves in court.

Acceptance also has some things to say to the daughter:

Everyone has trouble. Nobody escapes problems. Everyone has circumstances they don't like. Stop requiring everyone around you to live a perfect life. No one has a perfect life—so quit thinking you're entitled to one. The reality is that people you love will make decisions you don't like. In your case your mother has decided to leave your family, and her departure has hurt you deeply. But she's gone, and that's the way it is. From now on your mother will be living apart from your father and you will be traveling back and forth between households. You are now going to have to Accept what has happened.

Whether you like it or not, *what you do to your mother you do directly to yourself* because you are half your mother. If you speak against your mother, reject her, or hate her, you will only speak against yourself, reject yourself, and hate yourself.

So stop launching into your list of grievances whenever your mother's name is mentioned. Quit rolling your eyes; quit being so mean and critical; quit being so arrogant; and quit being such a smart mouth—so entitled and so right about everything. Give your mother some slack. Give her some grace. This is your mother we're talking about. Give her the respect and honor that is due her as your mother.

Quit rolling your eyes; quit being so mean and critical;
quit being so arrogant; and quit being such a smart mouth—
so entitled and so right about everything.

The transformational power of Acceptance is beyond imagination.

If we stacked all the failures and faults of the mother on one side of a weight scale and put just one thing—Acceptance by the daughter—on the other side, Acceptance would outweigh and cancel out in the daughter's life all the bad influences and all the wrongs of her mom.

This is the incredible power of Acceptance.

What Acceptance will do for this daughter borders on the miraculous.

Is Acceptance fair? Is it reasonable? Is it just and equitable?

Not in the slightest.

Acceptance is completely unfair. Acceptance is basically demanding that the father let the mother break his heart, divide up their assets, and alter his life forever—without any criticism or opposition. And for his daughter, Acceptance is demanding that she let her mother depart from their home to discover new relationships and new lifestyles for herself without resistance.

Acceptance is not only unfair, it's outrageous!

But it will heal this daughter.

The bar of Acceptance has been set high, the challenge is difficult. Yet, the bar can be reached.

If the father and daughter can just take the first steps, if they can Accept the mother and her boyfriend, if they can begin to be kind to them, if they can be gracious to them, and if they can continue to grow in Acceptance toward them, their kindness and Acceptance will restore the life of this daughter—and father.

Acceptance is not only unfair, it's outrageous!
But it will heal this daughter.

What about when the other parent creates hardships for the kids? How does Acceptance work then?

"When we go over on weekends we hardly see our dad," her children complain to their mother. "We are left alone at his house while he and his girlfriend are always out somewhere." But the children agree that it is actually better for their dad to be away than to be at home. When he is there, the dad and his girlfriend usually lock themselves away in the dad's bedroom. The worst thing, according to the kids, is when the girlfriend tries to interact with them. They don't like her and make certain she knows it. Reacting to their disrespect, the girlfriend calls them brats and they usually end up in shouting matches.

The mother, appalled at what's going on over at the dad's house, called the father to voice her complaints. After one particularly heated exchange, the mother told her kids, "Your father's a jerk."

The children said in reply, "Yeah, mom, he sure is."

But Step 2: Acceptance needs to weigh in quickly.

Neglect by the father is bad enough for the kids without the mother inflicting *more* damage.

In the mother's mind, she believes she's right to tell her children the truth about their father. "Let's not deny the obvious," she says. And, she's glad her children agree with her.

Yet, by the mother calling their father a jerk and with the children in full agreement with their mother, she's dismantling her kids and is assisting them to dismantle themselves.

Acceptance says if we cannot change anything about our exes, if we cannot get relief for our kids, at least let us not *cause further damage* by encouraging their growing disrespect toward their other parent.

Acceptance says if we cannot change anythingabout our exes, if we cannot get relief for our kids, at least let us not cause further damage by encouraging their growing disrespect towards their other parent.

Remember my daughter's stepfather? Remember the time he disciplined her by screaming in her face and breaking things in front of her?

Was I just to Accept what was going on with him? Was I just to Accept him treating my daughter this way?

Of course not. I did what I could, which was to seek a change in custody in Parent War 4—but I lost!

How was I to respond now?

One thing I should not have done was to *add* to my daughter's troubles by training her to carry animosity and disrespect toward both her mother and stepfather.

She had enough difficulties already without me compounding them.

From my standpoint was Acceptance fair or just? Not in the slightest. But it would have helped my daughter immeasurably.

This is Step 2: Acceptance. Acceptance means that you are to accept life as it is now handed to you. It means to Accept your separation, the fact that you now have an ex, and the reality that your children are going to be raised between two households. It means to Accept your ex's partner, the partner's children and family, and to allow them, with safeguards in place, into your life and your children's lives.

STEP 3: AMNESIA

After suffering through betrayal and emotional loss and a lengthy divorce, one father questioned why his ex-wife was being so generously rewarded by the court. The mediator and attorneys made sure that she got a liberal share of his assets, substantial alimony, and generous visitation with their children. He questioned the entire legal system. Why was she so favored in the eyes of the court? She was the one who betrayed her vows—not him. She was the one who devastated him and his children—not him. He wondered, don't vows mean anything? Isn't there a penalty for unfaithfulness?

He wondered, don't vows mean anything?
Isn't there a penalty for unfaithfulness?

Fast-forward a few years.

It came to light that this father had some past financial investments that had not been disclosed during the divorce proceedings. He had worked hard to build up his private portfolio believing that the assets were exclusively his and his ex was not entitled to any of the money.

His ex-wife took him back to court, calling him a liar and a cheat, demanding her rightful share of the money. She also demanded, and got, attorney fees.

The man was devastated. He had primary care of his kids and was already paying nearly all their expenses. Even if his ex was legally entitled to the money, he reasoned, it was still terribly unjust for her to go after it.

But things only got worse. A few days after the settlement, the mom shows up at his house to pick up the kids for her regular visitation and they're thrilled to see her. It was baffling to him. The courts had been clearly supportive of this woman and so are his kids! His ex is getting her way in everything.

To the dad, this woman does not deserve the love of her children. He believes that if they knew the truth about their mother, they would not be so welcoming of her.

Yet, Step 3, Amnesia, has some requirements for this father.

Amnesia means for this father to never again view his ex as having committed any treacheries against him.

It's the father no longer rehearsing all the faults of his ex to himself or others.

It's this dad putting away all his anger, hurt, and sorrow.

It's never again forcing his children into his adult world by informing them of his private difficulties with their mother.

What was the worst thing that happened to this father because of this lawsuit? The father lost some money.

But what is the worst thing that can happen to the children if they learn about the lawsuit? Their structures could be cracked up for years to come.

The father's loss is momentary. His children's loss can be for a lifetime.

The father will recover from his loss. If informed, his children may never recover from theirs.

The temporary satisfaction the father might gain by telling his children the faults of their mother pale in comparison to the years of heartbreak he will have to endure as he watches his children struggle in their lives.

Amnesia demands that the father take the unjust outcome of this recent lawsuit with him to the grave.

The father's loss is momentary.
His children's loss can be for a lifetime.

Certainly there are things parents must never forget—things that the ex may do that harm their children—so that the necessary safeguards can be put in place for the kids.

But Amnesia demands that everything else, all the past hurts and pains, must be put away and never brought up again.

But aren't parents being untruthful to their children if they allow them to believe in the goodness of a terrible parent?

One divorced mother told me her adult daughter recently became aware of some outrageous behaviors of her father toward her mother twenty years earlier. The daughter was angry with her mother for not telling her. She felt lied to, and hotly objected that she had innocently cared for her father, not knowing the truth about him.

But the mother replied, "I saved you by not telling you. What your father did, he did mainly to me. This was my grief and mine alone to bear. Because I kept the information from you, you remained close to your father and are the woman you are today. But be careful. Now that you know some of the things he did, you are responsible to continue to care for your father as if you never knew this information. Years ago I put these difficulties away. Now, you need to put them away for yourself."

Where is the rule that parents have to reveal every private thing between them to their kids?

Why all this 'openness' and 'honesty' about the other parent?

Aren't children naturally reactive? Isn't everything to them right or wrong? Don't they naturally take sides? Yet it's this reactive nature that structurally harms a child if directed toward a parent.

The daughter is wrong in thinking she needs to know all about her father's faults. The mother did the right thing in remaining silent, and in doing so helped to preserve her daughter's internal structure. *What children do to a parent they do directly to themselves.*

But isn't our painful past too deep and too devastating to be forgotten? How can we ever forget what our ex has done to us and to our children?

But isn't our painful past too deep and too devastating to be forgotten? How can we ever forget what our ex has done to us and to our children?

One separated parent sympathized with me that it must have been hard for me to dredge up all my past events and emotions for the sake of this book.

I told the parent that writing this book wasn't difficult at all. Years ago I had put away most of the troubling emotions of my Wars with my ex because Amnesia promised that if I did, it would restore my kids.

The problem for me was, back when I began to rid myself of my terrible memories, I discovered that I actually liked them.

Recalling my ex's failures made sense of my world.

It justified me. It told me that my ex caused my children's difficulties—that I was right and she was wrong. Plus I got a lot of mileage out of vocalizing my sufferings to friends and family. In return I got validation, affirmation, and sympathy.

But pursuing Amnesia ended all of this.

In the beginning I found it difficult to quit making mental lists of all her failures. It was hard to stop the negative comments to my children about their mother. I had to cease issuing regular updates to my friends. It took some effort for my wife and me to replace negative things with positive things. But we began telling my kids good stories about their mom.

And it worked.

Amnesia began restoring our kids.

This is Step 3: Amnesia. Amnesia means to put away the *negative emotions* of the past, and to treat the other parent as if there has never been a problem between you. Amnesia is to never inform your children of the difficulties you have suffered because of their other parent.

STEP 4: MERCY

Early in my work, when I was still developing the Seven Steps, I was approached by a very unhappy mother, a woman in her late sixties. As she described her terrible ex to me, I remember observing the strain lines etched on her face and her deep anguish. My heart went out to her.

Yet, standing beside her was her adult daughter, showing no signs of trouble or unhappiness. She had a pleasant expression on her face and was quite composed and relaxed. I was surprised at the contrast between the mother and her daughter.

The daughter, clearly doing well in her life, told me that her father was pretty cruel to her mom during their time of separation and continues to be unkind to the mom. But the daughter sees her father regularly and they get along well.

It was something to watch the mother noticeably wince in pain as her daughter spoke well of her father. I saw her struggle under the weight of her daughter's kind words about the dad.

It was something to watch the mother noticeably wince in pain as her daughter spoke well of her father.

It was obvious that the mother saw herself as right and the dad wrong, and that she clearly wanted her daughter to join with her against the father. Her anxiety over her daughter not taking her side against the father was physically oppressing her. The mother could not comprehend why her daughter continued to have anything to do with this terrible man.

But the daughter told me that her dad wasn't perfect, that he definitely had his problems, but she still loved her father and she would continue to see him regularly.

I stood there amazed at what the daughter had just said.

This daughter fulfilled Step 4: Mercy, and she fulfilled it perfectly.

This woman in her mid-thirties, clearly aware of her father's faults, clearly recognizing the horrible realities of his past, still clearly loved her father.

Wow. That's Mercy.

Mercy is this daughter recognizing her father's failures— and then adding a *but*, *still*, *yet*, or *nevertheless,* followed by expressions of care and love for her parent.

She said, "I know my father has his problems *but* I love him anyway."

It is her giving Mercy that launched this daughter into incredible emotional health. In giving her father Mercy she gave herself Mercy. In not taking up disappointments and criticisms against him, she didn't take up any disappointments and criticisms against herself. In caring for her father she cared for the father half of herself. This is the amazing work of Mercy in this daughter.

She said, "I know my father has his problems
but I love him anyway."

Here's how others have expressed this same Mercy:

"Every time I'm with my dad he's with another girlfriend. My mom hates my dad, *but* I love him and I still want to see him."

"My mom has had a difficult life and is a hard person to get along with, *but* I care for her. Because of her constant criticisms I'm forced to limit my time with her, *yet* I know she likes it when I visit her."

"My mom left my dad and is now with someone else. Everyone hates my mom and criticizes her. *Nevertheless,* I still care for my mother and try to see her as much as possible."

"My father is in prison and I regularly go to see him. Since my mom and dad are now divorced, my mom won't have anything more to do with him. *Still*, I care for my father and see some really good things about him."

These words—*but* or *still* or *yet* or *nevertheless*—followed by expressions of Mercy are what will create profound change in children. Any child, young or old, can discover this transforming experience when these powerful words are inserted into the conversation.

What about difficult parents—really difficult parents, parents who are hurtful to their children?

I know lots of them.

One time I asked a father why he never contacted his son. His reply to me: "The boy has his mother."

Another parent arranged to fly his two teenage daughters from their mother's home to the city where he now lives to personally say goodbye, as he planned never to see them again. He told them to no longer consider him their father and to not try to contact him. When putting them back on the plane, he said to both daughters, "Have a great life."

One woman has a mother who is very demanding, very

hurtful, and deeply critical of her. Spending any time with her mother always leaves the daughter an emotional wreck.

And then there's the father who can only see his children under supervised visitation because he has physically abused them.

How are children to show Mercy toward parents like these?

Nothing changes.

Structural injury occurs when kids carry hatred, criticism, complaint, and negative reaction toward a parent. Structural health can never come out of ongoing negative responses toward a parent, no matter how awful that parent and no matter how justified the children.

Even with kids who have the necessary boundaries and safeguards set in place, even with kids who have been physically separated—even permanently separated—for their protection, children must still be Merciful.

If children are to become emotionally transformed, they must add a *but, still, yet,* or *nevertheless* to all the failures of a parent.

Positive responses are the only way children will ever be structurally restored.

Positive responses are the only way children will ever be structurally restored.

I know one situation where a father sexually abused his daughter for years while her mother did nothing to prevent it. Twenty years later, with no contact between the woman and her parents and still deeply troubled and damaged, the woman knew that to be freed from her incredibly difficult past required her to forgive them and give up her bitter memories.

This meant that she would have to contact them. Following an exchange of cards and phone calls she and her husband went to see her parents. Even though it was a grueling experience for her, she forced herself to face her unspeakable past and gave her parents Mercy.

By adding a *but*, *still*, *yet*, or *nevertheless* followed by Acceptance and kindness to her parents, she experienced a level of internal peace and happiness that she would never have had without Mercy.

The reality is children were never designed to wage war against a parent. They're not built to hate or malign a parent. Children are too biologically integrated with their parents. *What children do to their parents, they do directly to themselves.*

Children are designed to be *only merciful* toward both parents, to give them a break, to let things go, to forget an offense, and to be gracious. If there are any punitive measures to be given, if there are any judgments or disciplinary actions to be measured out, they must come from outsiders—anyone but the children.

---

*The reality is children were never designed
to wage war against a parent.*

I was speaking about Mercy at a conference and one individual said, "That's all we need to do—just love one another."

But that is not what Mercy is saying.

Can children criticize irresponsible behaviors? Absolutely.

Should they condemn criminal activity? Of course. Can children oppose people hurting other people? Most certainly.

But Mercy is saying children cannot *carry* these verdicts against *their own* parents.

I saw a news report about a businessman convicted of financial fraud. The video showed him standing before a judge about to be sentenced. And directly behind him were his adult children who were there in support of their father. I thought, how perfect, this is exactly what should happen. The court is giving out judgment to a guilty man, yet his children are with him. They recognize their father's failures, yet they are standing united with him and committed to him. The kids are not approving of their father's actions but remain approving of him.

This is Step 4: Mercy, and this is exactly what these children need to do—and exactly what every child needs to do with both parents—regardless of the parents' behaviors.

Wouldn't it be something to see children stand by their mom who had destroyed their family?

Or, what about children standing alongside their dad, now with his fourth live-in girlfriend, whose irresponsible behaviors have negatively affected the children's lives?

It is these acts of Mercy toward their parents that will propel children into incredible emotional health.

So, how is a parent to respond when children see their other parent's failures?

One mom told me that her ex is irresponsible and terrible and her children know it. She asked, "What am I to do? Lie to them and tell them everything's okay?"

I told her that children see parent problems all the time. But it is their negative conclusions about their parent that will cause them structural damage.

The question the Principles ask is, "After your children see their other parent's failures, and after you and your children talk, and after everything is said and done, what's the final conclusion? Are there any expressions of care and support toward that offending parent?"

"What am I to do? Lie to them and tell them everything's okay?"

With Principle Two alone children can significantly launch themselves into emotional health: *What children do to their parents they do directly to themselves.*

This is Step 4: Mercy. Mercy is recognizing a parent's failures but adding a *but, still, yet,* or *nevertheless,* followed by expressions of care and love for that parent. Children are not designed to measure out justice or issue verdicts or penalties toward their own parents: They are only designed to give them Mercy.

STEP 5: NEUTRAL—DAMAGING

As the car pulled up to his mom's house the ten-year-old reached into the backseat one last time to pet his dad's family dog. Then, opening the car door and saying goodbye to his dad, he grabbed his backpack and hopped out.

Watching his father drive away the boy immediately became all business. Walking up the stone pathway toward his mom's house he had some urgent work to do with only seconds to spare.

The problem was that he and his dad, stepmom, and stepsister had just returned from a terrific four-day vacation at their family cabin and they all had a great time together, making his job even more difficult than normal. Going back to his mom's house meant that he had to forget everything that happened at his dad's.

---

*Going back to his mom's house meant that he had to
forget everything that happened at his dad's.*

Which meant the entire trip had to go.

The first had to be the dog! He loved that dog, a golden retriever who never left his side the entire four days. He quickly threw that down to his right. Then there were the horses, especially Daniel, his favorite horse to ride. He tossed them alongside the dog. Third were the canoes and paddle boats at the lake. They were quickly discarded and littered behind him. Next, evening times at the cabin and the outdoor barbecuing. That was so much fun. But they all had to go.

On impulse he decided not to toss aside the bee sting. Boy, did that hurt! He and his dad were out in the canoe paddling up a creek and around some big bushes when a bee flew out and stung him on the foot. It hurt sooo badly but his dad quickly put some ice from the cooler on the area and it helped a lot. The boy knew he was taking a big chance telling his mom about the bee sting—since it happened with his dad—but it was his first bee sting! It was too important—he had to tell her. But he knew to leave out the part about his dad and the ice from the cooler.

The entire four-day trip was quickly scattered at his feet, and just in time, as he was now about to open the front door.

Job done! Piled up behind him were four days of life with his dad, the dad half of himself cast aside and lying along the stone pathway up to the front door.

Stepping inside the house the boy had completely transformed himself into his other half, his mom's half, just the way his mom liked him—well, all except for the bee sting—but that was a risk he was willing to take.

He knew the rules. He had learned years ago that the things that went on over at his dad's stayed at his dad's and the things that went on at his mom's stayed at his mom's. Back then if he said anything to either his mom or dad about the other house, it ended badly, with one parent angry, saying harsh words about the other. So he learned to keep quiet about the other side. Today, even though his parents no longer speak against each other, he still doesn't say anything. If information about the other household does manage to get out, it's met with dead silence. It's clear that neither parent wants to know anything about the other parent, as there is no response, no questions, and no interest expressed.

And once again it proved true regarding the bee sting.

When the boy entered the house he was warmly greeted by his mom. She asked him how he was and he said he was fine. But with measured enthusiasm he told her a bee stung him on the foot while he was canoeing up a river. True to form his mom asked him if he was all right and he said he was and then she asked him to put all his dirty clothes in the laundry room and come into the kitchen to get something to eat. So that was it. Feeling disappointed—but as expected—an abrupt end to a cool bee-sting story.

In the mom's mind she's a great mom.

Upon learning about Principle One and Principle Two, the mom believes she is following the rules perfectly. Haven't she and her ex ceased all negative responses toward each other? Isn't she supportive of her son seeing his dad? And, isn't she building up the mom side and isn't the dad building up the dad side of their son? So she takes great satisfaction in believing her son is fine.

But her son is not fine.

She takes great satisfaction in believing her son is fine.
But her son is not fine.

The mom thinks that being Neutral toward the father— meaning there are zero positive and zero negative responses— has no effect on her son.

But it's her Neutral responses toward her son's father that are damaging her son. Because nothing positive is going on between the mom half and the dad half within the boy, he is left with this huge internal void.

This mom cannot bypass Principle One and get away with it: *What the mom does to the father she does directly into the heart of her son.*

Structural health will take place in the boy when his mom responds positively to the father half of her son.

How healthy it would be if his mom welcomed every aspect of her son's life.

She could be excited to hear about her son paddling with his dad up the river and him swimming around the island. She could wince with him at the bee sting and hear all about the ice and how it made it feel okay. And she could savor with him the nightly barbecuing which he loved so much.

Plus, there is another way this mother is putting her son in deep peril.

She has ceased managing how her son responds toward his father.

She has left the decision to him. If her son chooses to be positive or negative toward his father, it's his choice. If he decides to be Neutral toward him, that's okay with the mom, too.

By her Neutral responses the mom has placed the future emotional health of her child squarely into his hands, the hands of a ten-year-old.

---

*By her Neutral responses the mom has placed
the future emotional health of her child squarely into
his hands, the hands of a ten-year-old.*

Fortunately for the boy, things are going okay. He has a great relationship with his father. But this will likely change. Disagreements with his father and stepmother will arise. The dad siding with the stepmother in opposition to the son is bound to happen. And, the likelihood of the son retaliating by poor behavior and emotional withdrawal is also a common possibility. Principle Two says, *What a child does toward a parent directly impacts the child.*

If this boy is left to himself to determine his own level of response toward his father, the potential is very high that he will cause himself some emotional damage.

What this mother must do now is take back control of her son's responses, seeing to it that he always responds well toward his father.

The boy's internal structural health is too important, too valuable, and too critical to be left in the hands of a child.

The boy's internal structural health is too important, too valuable, and too critical to be left in the hands of a child.

But this is exactly what I did with my son.

When my son came to live with me, he had little to do with his mom. And I gave him my full support.

Fortunately for us, the mother went quiet, too. We rarely heard from her—maybe a couple of times a year.

What a gift it was for all of us to basically forget about her.

And things were going along great for my son at our home. He had a great relationship with his siblings and especially with my wife, his stepmother, whom he cared for deeply. School was going well and he excelled in sports.

To me, my son now had everything he needed to mature into a wonderful, stable adult. And, equally important, his mother and I were no longer at war.

So everything should have been fine, right?

But everything wasn't fine.

The mother half of my son was slowly becoming more and more internally damaged and I didn't know it—nobody knew it.

It turns out that I was the one who was emotionally damaging my son. Silently and steadily I was contributing to the breakdown of his internal structure.

I didn't even know it was possible for my son to become emotionally damaged at our home. He was thriving and doing so well. But by my lack of positive responses toward his mother, I lacked positive responses toward half my son. And, with my son neutral toward his mother he was also neglecting half himself.

Did I ever try to see that my son responded positively toward his mother? Did I ever encourage my son to call his mother or encourage him to go down and spend time with her? Did I ever remind him to acknowledge his mother's birthday or urge him to visit her on holidays? Not in the slightest.

Even though my son managed to see his mother a couple of times a year, it wasn't because of me.

How was it possible for my son to have an intact internal structure with half of it ignored?

But weren't his mother and I finally at peace? Wasn't zero contact with each other a good thing? I thought our Neutral responses were the best for everyone.

My poor son!

If I had understood the Two Principles and the importance of my behavior and his behavior toward his mother, I could have taken aggressive action toward making peace with her. I could have talked favorably about his mother to him. I could have arranged for him and his mother to get together. I could have taken the initiative to make sure that she felt welcomed in my home, welcomed to sit with me during our son's sports games, and welcomed to attend his school functions with me. And I could have seen to it that my son also responded favorably toward his mother.

These positive actions would have been difficult for me, but I could have gotten through the tough parts. I could have paid the price for my son's future. His mother and I could have made peace.

But weren't his mother and I finally at peace?
Wasn't zero contact with each other a good thing?

The problem is many separated parents have trouble imagining anything positive about their exes.

"Positive responses would simply encourage my children's father to continue to be irresponsible and self-centered."

"It's better to leave things as they are now with no mention of the other parent."

"Approval of the mother would encourage my children to act like her and that would be wrong."

"I have nothing positive to say about my ex."

But Neutral—Damaging is not about *partially* rebuilding damaged kids. It's about full and complete restoration. Neutral responses between parents tear down internal structures in kids.

Positive responses are the only thing that will rebuild their internal framework.

This is Step 5: Neutral—Damaging. Neutral—Damaging recognizes that only positive responses between parents, and positive responses between children and parents, build stable internal structures in children. Any other kind of response—Neutral or negative—will continue to damage kids.

STEP 6: BENEFITING

What would you do?

You're a single mom and your teenage daughter and younger son live primarily with you. You were treacherously abandoned by your now ex-husband and have grieved over his early remarriage to a woman he had been seeing while still married to you. What makes matters worse is the woman your ex has married is financially quite secure, so they live together in a beautiful home with a nice swimming pool and drive nice cars.

Along with your own personal trauma, your children are also shocked and deeply distressed at what their father did and to this point both have sided with you against him.

Recently your two children were invited by their father and his new wife to spend a summer week at her lakeside vacation home and go wake-boarding behind her ski boat. This is during your time with your children and you can easily say no. The kids are hesitant to show their excitement about the vacation. In fact, in support of you, your fourteen-year-old daughter has decided to stay home, but your son wants to go. The children don't know what to do or how to act and are looking to you for answers. What are you going to say to them and what are you going to do?

*The children don't know what to do or how to act
and are looking to you for answers.*

Step 6: Benefiting has some things to say.

You will tell your children to go with their father and his wife on vacation and enjoy themselves. In fact, you are going to insist that the children care for their father and stepmother, listen to them, be courteous to them, and accept the stepmom into their lives.

Furthermore, not only are you going to require your children to have a great time but you're also going to take them shopping to purchase some snacks and sports drinks for everyone to enjoy while driving up to the lake. And, when the children return from their vacation, you will take the time to listen to all their stories, enjoy all the photos, and be interested in all the activities that took place.

Principle One: *What you do to the other parent you do to your kids.*

In fact, you are going to insist that the children care for their father and stepmother…

This is Step 6, Benefiting.

Benefiting means complimenting the ex and the ex's partner.

It's saying thank-you.

It's inviting your ex to join you at your son's football games.

It's saying to a neglectful parent, "I'm glad you're here," even if the parent hasn't seen the children in months.

It's being generous with visitation schedules. It's allowing your children to travel freely between households.

It's going with your children to pick out birthday and holiday cards and gifts for their other parent and partner.

It's creating a welcoming environment for your ex and companion when they come to pick up the kids.

It's doing good things for the other parent in front of your kids.

It's working toward peace even if the other parent won't—even if the other parent is unworthy, arrogant, resistant, or inflexible.

It's accepting the negative actions of the ex without a negative response back from you.

It's working toward peace even if the other parent won't—even if the other parent is unworthy, arrogant, resistant, or inflexible.

Benefiting is also not shying away from attending various functions just because the other parent may show up.

I know how sitting with an ex feels. It's uncomfortable and weird and I've felt it a thousand times. Walking toward the sports field and seeing the ex sitting in the bleachers causes us to react. Don't we all find great relief when we know the other parent won't be there? We feel like we've been handed a summer vacation.

But what gives us relief is hard on our kids. Some discomfort for us today will pay great dividends for our children tomorrow.

Don't we all find great relief when we know the other parent won't be there? We feel like we've been handed a summer vacation.

Benefiting is not making a big show of your positive attitudes.

One fellow enthusiastically told me how he and his wife 'benefit' his wife's ex by their happy and positive approach toward the other parent. During her son's baseball games they would greet the ex-husband and his wife with big smiles and loud voices and waving their hands. Laughing, this man told me the father barely waves back and that his new wife just glares at them.

But they weren't Benefiting the ex at all.

Actually, what they were doing was quite negative, creating tension and discomfort. They weren't serving the ex—they were serving themselves and using their 'positive behaviors' as a way to harass them.

Benefiting means to discover what's best for the ex, what makes the other parent and partner feel comfortable, and what pleases them. For this husband and wife it means that they should quit smiling and making all their noises and gestures. It means, instead, to do something as simple as giving a quick look, a quick smile, and sitting nearby.

They weren't serving the ex—they were serving themselves and using their 'positive behaviors' as a way to harass them.

Benefiting is getting through all the legal stuff as quickly as possible.

One woman with primary custody of her children wanted her ex to live close by so he could see their children more. But the ex couldn't afford the housing. So the woman and her second husband agreed to release the ex from several hundred dollars a month in child support if he would agree to live near them. Today the kids' dad is living in the same school district as the children and seeing them regularly. Imagine how well these children are doing!

This is true child support.

Answering her door, the single mom was handed a beautiful bouquet of flowers by a delivery florist. It was a gift for the mom's birthday.

Opening the card to see who they were from, her emotions suddenly ran cold. She couldn't believe her eyes. The flowers were a gift from her ex-husband, the man who had torn out her heart, the one who had betrayed their vows with all his girlfriends. And now he sends her flowers? After cutting her emotionally in half he's now saying, "Let's be friends"? What an insult. Did he actually believe sending flowers would make everything okay?

After cutting her emotionally in half
he's now saying, "Let's be friends"?

To this mom the only thing the flowers accomplished was to pour more salt on her wounds. Instead of something beautiful to grace her home the flowers were a reminder of her past terrible sufferings. Barely able to touch them she carried the bundle of flowers outside and threw them in the trash.

Here's the problem. The mom has just entered very dangerous territory.

I have met this woman. I am convinced that in time she will

let go of her awful past and relinquish her hurt. In time she and her ex will have a decent working relationship. In time she will recover.

But she's *out of time* with her kids!

What this mom is doing is what separated parents commonly do—take whatever time they need to get their lives back together. But when they finally do, their kids are a mess. The parents are fine. They have moved on. But their children are left broken, defeated, isolated, emotionally stuck back in those painful years, struggling with difficult behaviors, immature, and incapable of handling the responsibilities that come with age.

This mom's children should not have to wait for their mother to process through her separation. They need her to respond positively to their father and they need her to do it *now*.

Upon discovering who sent the flowers, the mom should have told her children that the flowers were a gift from their father for the mother's birthday, telling them how nice it was for their father to have sent them.

In honoring the father's gift she would have honored and supported the internal framework of her children: *What she does to the father she does directly to the structure of her kids.*

Would this be hard for the mom?

Absolutely. But the mom must be committed to the task. It's Benefiting her ex today that will build structural health in her kids.

One parent declared that Step 6: Benefiting doesn't apply in her case.

After she and her ex split up he moved out of the country, planning never to return. With her ex completely out of the way, the mom believes she has no reason to ever speak about this man again.

Plus, the mom feels it's best for her and her daughter to move on and to quit living in the past.

With her ex completely out of the way, the mom believes she has no reason to ever speak about this man again.

But the Principles are adamant.

No matter what, this daughter will continue to be half her father—meaning that he remains key to her structural stability and needs to be respected as a critical part of her life.

Yes, the mother and daughter can get on with their lives.

Yes, they can move forward—which likely includes a new partner for the mom and, in the future, great relationships for the daughter.

Yet, moving forward doesn't mean ignoring or getting rid of the father. In fact, just the opposite. It's the mother giving her daughter a good image of her father that will settle the young girl and give her the internal framework to have a full life.

Benefiting for this mom means telling her daughter good stories about her father.

It's providing her daughter with some sort of a positive rationale of why her father left so she can continue to think well of him.

This is Step 6: Benefiting. Benefiting means to do good to the ex and the ex's new family, now! It's setting the example for your children. It's behaving as if you are healed from your difficult past with your ex.

STEP 7: THE COST OF DOING BUSINESS

The problem is, while we are trying to fulfill the Two Principles and the Steps and trying to respond positively to our exes, our exes are probably not trying to do the same back to us.

Has this happened to you?

You speak well of the other parent but your ex continues to slander you.

You greet your ex at your son's birthday party but your ex won't give you the time of day.

You stand near your ex at one of your children's soccer games and your ex makes some critical comments about your new dating partner.

You have to cancel one of your kid's orthodontia appointments and, as a courtesy, you call your ex but all you get is anger and criticism.

You have been flexible changing weekends with your ex, but when you need your ex to make a change, the ex refuses.

You get the idea. You're changing your responses for the better, but your ex has no interest in changing theirs toward you. In fact, your ex continues to be rude and offensive and has no intention of making peace.

---

*You speak well of the other parent but
your ex continues to slander you.*

One couple complained that the wife's ex is always late to pick up his son. He is not just late but chronically late, sometimes hours late. The dad's irresponsible behavior is embittering them against him causing them to complain about the dad to this boy.

They are stuck with an ex who is inconsiderate and obnoxious, willfully trying to cause them all the trouble he can, and they are at a loss as to what to do.

This couple is experiencing what we call 'The Cost of Doing Business.' Since the father won't change his behavior, The Cost of Doing Business for this couple means that they will have to change theirs. Adapting to the ex will be the price they will have to pay to bring peace into this very aggravating situation.

It is upon this couple to modify their schedules and adjust their expectations so that when the ex does show up late, nobody cares. The couple must neutralize the impact of the father's chronic behavior and arrange things so that the father being late is no longer an issue.

Having adapted to the father and having minimized the impact of his obstinate behavior, they will be able to better preserve the emotional health of the son. What is *not* acceptable is for this couple to continue the way things are now, to continue to complain, get angry, and rehash all the faults of the other parent.

What is not *acceptable is for this couple to continue the way things are now, to continue to complain, get angry, and rehash all the faults of the other parent.*

If they don't adapt to the father but continue to criticize him, they will jeopardize the emotional health of the boy.

I know the couple, and unfortunately they're not even trying to adjust to the father. They continue to carry animosity toward him and to deeply criticize him to his son.

"Look how self-centered and inconsiderate he is," they would say. "What a failure. He can't even manage his own life."

"Why should we have to change? He's the one who's irresponsible. He's the one creating all the problems. Why should we have to adapt to him?"

"Why should we have to change?
He's the one who's irresponsible.
He's the one creating all the problems.
Why should we have to adapt to him?"

To hear the couple's story, to hear about all their misery and all the hardships they've had to endure because of this self-centered father—Oh my gosh, aren't they so right. How perfect they are. How responsible and timely they are. They're not late nor have they ever been late.

But look how damaging they are to this son!

The boy doesn't have a chance.

The problem is these 'excellent' parents have all the right answers. Isn't what they are saying true? Isn't being chronically late wrong? And if the boy tries to stand up and defend his father, isn't he defending irresponsible behavior? Look at what will happen to the boy. Upon him will descend all this 'righteous' disapproval. In defending his father, he is then emotionally destroyed by his mother and stepfather. It's a battle the boy will never win.

How right this 'good' couple is. But how destructive they are.

How right this 'good' couple is. But how destructive they are.

What a surprise it would be for these parents to learn that it is they, and not the dad, who have become agents of injury to the boy. In speaking against the dad this couple is speaking directly against the son. *What they do to the dad they do directly to the structure of the twelve-year-old.*

And look at the results. Years later the boy is a mess.

We've seen these same types of conflicts take place a hundred times—an ex obstinate over money, discipline, driving, clothes, what their kids eat, even how they comb their kid's hair *with the 'good' parent refusing to adapt.*

One pre-school daughter came running up to her mom after a weekend with her father, all excited about her new outfit and her new hair style and makeup. To the sheer delight of this young girl, her father's girlfriend had spent the afternoon giving her a complete makeover.

The mother stood there in shock. The clothes were indecent, her hair style inappropriate. She was aghast at the makeup—for a four year old?—and horrified that this other woman had even touched her daughter. The mother already highly objected to her ex and girlfriend's over-emphasis on clothes and appearance but to influence her daughter in this same way was something this mom could not bear.

Furious with her ex, she told him in no unmistakable terms that her daughter was never to wear those kinds of clothes again and that she, the mother alone, would determine her daughter's hairstyle and any future makeup.

Things only went downhill from there.

Hearing from the dad about the mom's objections, the girlfriend became incensed. She knew the objections were a direct attack against her. If anyone else dressed up her daughter, the mother wouldn't have minded one bit. But she knew the mother's hostility was leveled directly against her as the 'evil' live-in girlfriend.

So, two weekends later, having done the child's laundry prior to returning the little girl to her mom's, the girlfriend inserted into the stack of clean clothes some sensual women's underwear.

The mom went ballistic. The girlfriend, of course, was mystified as to how they got there. The mother knew exactly what this woman had done. When her ex arrived the next week to pick up his daughter, the mom threw the underwear in his face, screaming at him that he and his girlfriend were worthless and immoral human beings. She told her ex he could forget about seeing his daughter this weekend and that if he didn't like it he could just take her to court—then slammed the door in his face. The mom determined that no matter what it took, her daughter would never see this girlfriend again, even if it meant preventing her daughter from seeing her father. Standing in the entry way of her home the mother wept bitterly, overwhelmed with unhappiness and heartache, and so did her young daughter, terribly confused and distraught over her mother's deep distress.

...the mom threw the underwear in his face,
screaming at him that he and his girlfriend
were worthless and immoral human beings.

But The Cost of Doing Business has some things to say to this mother.

This incident has gone completely out of control. You need an entirely new way to deal with your ex and his girlfriend.

So what if your ex's dating partner wants to play house by dressing up your daughter, doing her make-up, and styling her hair?

How about enjoying the attention and fun your daughter was having?

Couldn't you have said something nice to the dad like, "Well, it looks like you guys have been busy over the weekend." Then, without making a fuss or saying anything negative, couldn't you have changed your daughter's clothes, washed out her hair, and removed her makeup during her bath—and be done with it?

But now everything has escalated. It has gone from objecting to the girlfriend dressing up your daughter, to anger against the father, to retaliation by the girlfriend, to threats of the child never seeing the girlfriend again, to separating the daughter from her father.

What is structural health in your daughter worth? *What parents do to each other they do directly to their kids.*

What is structural health in your daughter worth?

But we cannot leave this discussion without asking the question: What is The Cost of Doing Business with us?

Are we forcing our exes to adapt to our difficult behaviors?

Are we late? Are we argumentative? Are we disrespectful? Are we unkind or rude? Have we slandered our ex's new family? Do we become angry on the phone? Do we carry grudges? Do we refuse to swap weekends? Are we disagreeable about letting our kids be with their other parent?

One woman's ex was having huge conflicts with her over the way she disciplined their children. She strongly believed in spanking her kids, but her ex opposed any type of physical punishment. In fact, he told the mother that if she ever spanked their children again, he would call Child Protective Services and take them away from her.

But because her children lived primarily with her, the mother believed that she alone had the right to determine how they were to be raised. The mother resented her ex's opposition, claiming that he was intruding into her personal life. And she was not going to be bullied by him. In her eyes she was the good parent and her ex, the bad parent. He was the one who was being controlling and manipulative and overstepping his boundaries.

But the problem is not with the ex but with this mom.

Come on. The dad's demands are not unreasonable. There are a number of excellent ways to discipline children without spanking them.

It was this mom standing her ground and demanding her way that prevented peace between her and her ex. She was requiring her ex to adapt to her. *She was forcing her ex to pay The Cost of Doing Business with her.*

The Parent Wars that are sure to escalate over this dispute will likely prove extremely damaging to the children.

I know exactly what I'm talking about.

I was purposely a terrible ex-spouse. My ex-wife had caused me so much suffering it was a relief to get some payback. But it never occurred to me that my behavior fell directly on my kids.

For two decades I refused any input from my ex. I cut off all discussion with her. To me, my ex was completely incapable of any rational thought or any responsible action. I strongly believed she had lost all rights to parenting and should be the one to pay a heavy emotional price for separating from me.

So, when the opportunity arose, I purposely did things just to spite her. If she needed something from me, I refused. If she needed a favor, I was too busy. If I was the cause of her losing time at work, I was pleased. If I was the reason behind heated arguments between her and her husband, I felt a sense of accomplishment. If I negatively impacted her schedule, caused her to miss appointments, or forced her to pay extra money, I didn't mind one bit. She would throw a fit of anger and I would think, "Hey. Life's tough. Deal with it. I hope you're miserable."

But for the structural stability of my children, I should have been the one to adapt, to be agreeable, and to change. Instead of being a bad ex, I needed to have become a good ex.

She would throw a fit of anger and I would think,
"Hey. Life's tough. Deal with it. I hope you're miserable."

"But why is it always on me to have to make the changes," complained one parent, "Why do I have to be the one to always roll over and let my ex walk all over me?"

Another parent also complained, "I'm sick of being the one who has to give in to my ex. Why does he get to win?"

But the Principles ask us to forget about who gets their way.

When we do something peaceful and accepting towards our exes, that kindness will penetrate directly into our children's souls. Our actions of Acceptance and Mercy and Benefit will add a level of stability and maturity to our children that will amaze us.

Our actions alone can remarkably alter our children.

Another parent also complained, "I'm sick of being the one who has to give in to my ex. Why does he get to win?"

But what are we to do when the demands made by our exes are unreasonable?

During the years my ex had primary custody of our children she demanded that I do all the driving between our homes, one hour each way, all the pickups and drop-offs. She said if I wanted the kids, I could come and get them. To me she was being completely unreasonable. Yet, I gave in to her demands and did all the driving.

Another time she demanded an increase in child support but I resisted and successfully defended myself in court.

In one instance I gave in to her demands; in another I didn't give in at all. So the result is I don't think there is any one hard or fast rule as to when to oppose an ex or when to give in (except when providing safeguards for the kids).

Building peace in our children means for us, as much as possible, to quit our opposition, to quit standing our ground, to quit drawing lines in the sand, and to quit resisting the other parent.

And forget about things like equity and fairness between separated parents. They don't exist among separated parents anyway. Quit trying to make them exist.

Structural health in kids is only found among parents who adapt the most, endure the most, accept the most, and forget the most.

I know scores of parents who pay the extra money, buy the extra clothes, drive the extra miles, do all the pickup and dropping off, attend all the school functions, buy the extra sports equipment, oversee all the homework, and take time off from work for the kids without the other parent so much as lifting a finger to help.

These are the true heroes among separated parents. These are the true builders of structural health and maturity in their children.

This is Step 7: The Cost of Doing Business. The Cost of Doing Business is *adapting* to the difficult behaviors of the other parent and *enduring* hardship. It also means *making* peace for the sake of the stability of your kids.

PART 3

TRIUMPH

The incredible restoration of my daughter
to making good decisions, to healthy behaviors, and to
emotional stability

MY ATTEMPT TO MAKE PEACE WITH THE MOM

My poor daughter.

The time was just after Parent War 4 when I as yet knew nothing about the Two Principles or Seven Steps. I had lost in court because my thirteen-year-old daughter remained silent before a court counselor. The end result of that court battle was the hollowing out of our precious daughter as, over the next few years, she became completely incorrigible and defiant.

During these years my daughter and I barely saw each other. Yet, I knew I needed to do something. I was losing her.

And then a radical idea came to me.

Maybe I should stop opposing her mom. Maybe I should try extending an olive branch, and try to make peace with her mother for the sake of our daughter.

So far, resisting my ex and constantly criticizing her hadn't worked. It didn't take much to see that our Parent Wars had torn our daughter apart and had caused her great emotional difficulties.

The question was, how to begin?

Taking the first step would require me to call her mom and then meet with her.

Ugh. Not an easy task. The few conversations we'd had over the last years were filled with animosity. But my desperate concern about my daughter forced me to make the call.

After answering the phone and hearing my voice the mom went dead quiet. I told her I was concerned about our daughter and asked if we could meet together.

Her responses to me consisted of nothing more than one-word sentences. Yet she surprised me by agreeing to a meeting. I asked if a certain day and time were good and she gave a one-word affirmative.

So that was it—a few sentences from me and a couple of words from her and I was now going to actually have a meeting with the individual whom I still despised after all these years.

---

*…I was now going to actually have a meeting
with the individual whom I still despised after all these years.*

After opening her front door my daughter's mom didn't say a word. She just turned around, walked into her living room, and sat on a couch on the far side of the room. I walked in, closed the door, and sat as far from her as possible.

In my mind I didn't think I had ever seen anyone so filled with hatred. She just sat there, her face as cold as steel. Her eyes pierced through me. She sat stiff as a board on the edge of the couch, her neck and every back muscle rigid.

---

*She sat stiff as a board on the edge of the couch,
her neck and every back muscle rigid.*

I knew my daughter was there and I saw her in the hallway. It was clear that she was upset about my being over at her mom's house and wanted nothing to do with me or her mom in the same room.

But I called out to her and asked her to come and sit with us. I told her what I had to say was for both her and her mom.

Mad that she had been seen and madder yet that she had to join us, with a huge show of displeasure—tossing her head, rolling her eyes—she plopped down on a separate couch, swung her legs over the side, and turned her back to me.

But I wanted my fifteen-year-old to see what was about to take place. Since she was five years old she had not seen or heard me speak kindly to her mother. This was sure to be a dramatic new experience for her and me—for all of us—so I wanted it to count.

The atmosphere in the room felt thick with animosity. I couldn't imagine hatred overtaking my ex as much as it seemed to that evening. She just sat there glaring at me, not saying a word. My daughter, defiant, sat with her back to me.

The feelings were mutual. I didn't want to be there either.

But I had to begin.

I had to begin the long work of getting over our past and letting issues go and doing what I could to bring health back into my daughter.

I was waging a different kind of war now, a war against hatred and the internal destruction of my daughter.

I was waging a different kind of war now, a war against hatred and the internal destruction of my daughter. The weapons of my warfare this time were different from those I had used before. And, it was I who fired the first shot.

I apologized.

I said to my ex that it must have been awful going through so much hardship with our daughter. I acknowledged that it must have been difficult for her to have faced a rebellious daughter completely on her own, without any help from me. I apologized for not supporting her.

I told her I was finished being at war with her and that I was going to give her my full support. I said I was sorry that I had opposed her all these years and that from this time forward things were going to be different. I asked her to tell me how I could help her and said that I was willing to do whatever she asked.

As my ex listened to my apology, she didn't blink an eye. For most of our meeting, which didn't last long, she never moved a muscle. She sat ramrod straight in her chair with her face frozen, in what I can only describe as pure disgust.

That evening I behaved as if I knew all about the Two Principles and Steps, but I honestly didn't know a thing about them. Yet, I seriously determined right then and there that I would never speak against my children's mother again—nor would I criticize her to my kids or to anyone else.

I have to say that I was so busy concentrating on my own behavior and busy figuring out what I was going to say that I don't remember her response, if she ever said anything. Nor do I remember my daughter saying anything either.

I don't think we talked about anything else because our meeting was so short. And I don't recall how the meeting ended, although I do remember thinking that my ex's neck muscles seemed to have relaxed a little—but I could be wrong.

My daughter didn't know it, her mother didn't know it— heck, I didn't even know it—but the powerful initial stages of restoration and healing for my daughter had begun.

*My daughter didn't know it, her mother didn't know it—
heck, I didn't even know it—but the powerful initial stages
of restoration and healing for my daughter had begun.*

It is interesting to reflect back and note the irony of the situation, that healing had begun in a most unlikely venue—of all places, at the mom's home in an atmosphere that was to me filled with aggression and hatred.

All the time I was there everything seemed completely surreal. My own feelings were rebelling against me, my own mind opposed me, and everything inside me was telling me I was doing the wrong thing. Wasn't I the innocent person here? I was convinced our marriage failed because of her. I believed our children were messed up because of her. And here I was apologizing to her? My mind and my emotions objected to everything that was happening.

*...healing had begun in a most unlikely venue—
of all places, at the mom's home in an atmosphere that was
to me filled with aggression and hatred.*

But I was becoming more and more convinced that working *with* my kids' mother was the only solution to our daughter's instability. I had a sense I was on the right track and going in the right direction. I was determined to try peace, even going so far as to oppose my own feelings of right and wrong by humbling myself and apologizing to their mother.

So, with my daughter present, I gave her mother my full support—something I couldn't have imagined myself ever doing.
This wasn't about the mom at all but had everything to do with
the emotional health of my daughter. It was on behalf of my
children that I determined to treat their mother with her rightful
status of parent.

Sad to say, any peace that might have begun with that
meeting didn't last.

Whatever working relationship I gained by meeting with my
ex was immediately lost.

Restoration for my daughter that night was cut short by
the next two Parent Wars: War 5, initiated by my daughter, and
War 6, initiated by my son. Once these Wars began, everything
went downhill. Forget about trying to work with that woman. I
reverted back to hating her and having as little to do with her
as possible.

TRYING TO BUILD PEACE WITH MY DAUGHTER

Our continuing Parent Wars only made my daughter worse.

After Parent War 5 ended, and after living with me for only a couple months, my daughter ran away to live with a girlfriend and her family. Now sixteen years of age and fully self-emancipated, she and I again had very little contact.

Yet, I was desperately concerned for my very, very lost daughter. I knew that it was up to me to rebuild the relationship.

Yet, I was desperately concerned for my very, very lost daughter.

So I called her up and invited her out to dinner.

She wasn't anxious to meet with me and probably would have turned me down, but I quickly let her know that I wasn't interested in trying to correct her or try to improve her in the slightest. I told her I just wanted to be with her. I said she could talk to me about anything she wanted or say anything she wanted and I promised not to criticize her. So, under those conditions, she reluctantly agreed to see me. Heck, in her mind at least she'd get a free meal.

And the dinner went well. We had a good time and I kept up my part of the bargain. Yet, I hardly recognized her. Just seeing her broke my heart. She was someone I didn't even know. What my daughter looked like and how she talked shocked me, but I worked hard to cover up any disapproval. What else could I do? If I had reacted negatively, I'd have lost all contact with her. If I was to ever see her again, I needed to accept her as she was.

What my daughter looked like and how she talked shocked me...

So I made things between us as enjoyable as possible and hoped some good would come of it.

At the time I didn't realize how important it was for us to meet. Nor did I have a clue as to the healing that had begun deep within my troubled sixteen-year-old.

What happened next surprised me. She agreed to have dinner with me again.

And the next time we met, she agreed again. And again. What began with one dinner turned out to be nine months of dinners. Every Wednesday night my daughter and I ate together, and the value of our being together was priceless for both of us.

I would pick her up at the same time every Wednesday evening and take her to the same restaurant where we sat as much as possible in the same booth with the same server.

I was desperate to insert some consistency into my daughter's life. Everything else about her was in constant upheaval and change. So each week I tried to provide her with two hours of tradition and stability that she could absolutely count on.

I was thankful for every minute we had together and I made the most of our time, filling my daughter with positive response.

And I enjoyed being with her. But even better, she began to enjoy being with me. What I didn't know was that in learning to care for me, she was beginning to care for herself. In starting to respect me she was beginning to respect herself. In liking me, she began to like something deep inside herself. Little did I know that this time of positive response between us was what my daughter needed to begin to rebuild from the terrible devastation in her life.

In starting to respect me she was beginning to respect herself.
In liking me, she began to like something deep inside herself.

And I never corrected her.

The entire time we were together I listened to her and loved her. We talked about everything, *even her mother!* During these conversations I made it a point to speak well of her mom. In fact, it was the first time she ever heard good stories about her mother.

But none of this would have worked if I had not forced myself to forget our awful past. I made myself act as if nothing had ever happened between us.

I had to absolutely put out of my mind my daughter's objectionable behaviors during the years she lived at her mother's house and the couple of months at my home. I pushed away any memories of that awful lawsuit during Parent War 4 when she refused to speak with the mediator, causing me to lose my case and most of my custody. And, I had to put out of my mind how she rejected me and my home after Parent War 5, choosing instead to live with an out-of-control girlfriend.

Look at the turn of events.

Here I was meeting my daughter, hoping to be of some help to her, and here I was the one who was radically changing.

Here I was meeting my daughter, hoping to be of some help to her,
and here I was the one who was radically changing.

Actually, we were both changing. For the first time since her mother's and my divorce I was on the right track with my daughter. I didn't know it at the time but I was altering her very soul.

And, my daughter was beginning to trust me.

STILL MISSING THE MARK

Yes, I was building up the father side of my daughter by meeting with her regularly. And yes, I was doing some minor re-building of my daughter's mother side through telling her good stories about her mom.

But I was still a long way from full restoration of my daughter.

So again I decided to try to build some sort of peace with my ex.

Coming up was our son's high school graduation. I found the courage to actually invite his mom to his graduation ceremony—and she accepted my invitation.

This was really something. All during the time my son attended high school I'd had very little contact with his mother and here I was inviting her to his graduation—and she came.

...I'd had very little contact with his mother and here I was inviting her to his graduation—and she came.

Normally at past school functions I would sit on one side of the room with my ex on the other, and we would have separate celebrations following the event. This time, however, things were different. We actually sat near each other—and then she came to my home after the ceremony.

I couldn't believe it. My ex was actually attending a dinner celebration for our son in my home. Even though she and I hardly spoke to each other—still, this was remarkable.

And again, a few years later at my son's college graduation, everyone in our family gathered together at a large restaurant. My ex arrived with her family and I arrived with mine. Although there was little interaction between us throughout the evening, I thought that just being in the same room with my ex for three hours was very positive for my kids.

Only now can I look back and see that I fell seriously short of what was required of me to restore my children. Here I was congratulating myself on my 'positive' responses toward my ex, only to learn later that I had not even been close to effecting any real change in my son or daughter.

Here I was congratulating myself on my 'positive' responses toward my ex, only to learn later that I had not even been close to effecting any real change in my son or daughter.

I thought just stopping what caused emotional damage was what my daughter needed to return to emotional health. But stopping damage is one thing. Rebuilding is another.

I was learning that my daughter and son needed me to do more, a lot more.

Meeting with my children's mother in a room and ignoring her for two hours wasn't going to cut it.

What parents do to each other, they do directly to their kids.

A MOST UNEXPECTED RELATIONSHIP

What took place next surprised everyone.

My young son from my second marriage and my ex's son from her second marriage, both about the same age, met each other and became best friends. Realizing at a young age that they shared the same older brother and sister, they immediately declared themselves brothers. This close relationship continues to this day, with my son's 'brother' later becoming best man at my son's wedding!

Because of this friendship, contact with my ex took on a whole new turn. At this time both our daughter and son were living on their own so I had no reason to see my ex again. But soon my ex and I were driving half way between our homes to drop off or pick up my youngest son or hers.

Even my ex's husband shared in the driving! And my young son and this man got along great.

Can it get any weirder than this? I was seeing my ex and her husband regularly.

Can it get any weirder than this?

One summer my wife and I took the two boys on a rafting trip through Yosemite National Park. We had so much fun as we spent the entire day swimming and exploring every foot of the river.

When we returned my ex's son to his home a couple of

days later, he was filled with endless stories of our trip to Yosemite.

And our efforts were reciprocated. When my son stayed at my ex's house, he also had a great time.

How strange—here I was actually doing things for my ex's son and grateful for her being kind to my son. This seriously affected me. I actually appreciated my ex.

CHANGES TAKING PLACE WITH ME

After years of my working with separated parents the Principles and Steps finally became clear, giving me a distinct path toward restoring my children, especially my deeply troubled daughter.

Forget how my daughter dressed. Forget her heavy makeup. Forget her lifestyle. Forget her incoherent friends. Forget her failure in school. Forget that she was completely consumed with her own self-interest. No threats or appeals or any amount of discipline or coaxing from her mother or me could have caused my daughter to want to change her life.

My daughter needed her internal structure rebuilt. She needed internal restoration. She needed the wars raging within her to cease. She needed her parents to behave like parents, to treat each other with respect, and to bring her into maturity as parents should.

She needed her parents to behave like parents,
to treat each other with respect, and to bring her
into maturity as parents should.

Now with the Two Principles and Seven Steps I knew what to do. Finally, after nearly two decades, I began behaving as I should have behaved following my separation so many years earlier. I couldn't change my daughter, I couldn't change my ex, but I could change me.

I couldn't change my daughter, I couldn't change my ex,
but I could change me.

When I first began speaking well of my children's mother to my daughter and son, the effects were amazing. Each of them wore huge grins on their faces.

I told them how their mother was an excellent piano player, how she loved nature, was very brave with animals, very gifted in decorating, and on and on. I told them funny stories, respectful stories, stories of their mother's accomplishments and successes.

Both kids really liked the stories and would ask a lot of questions. I was surprised by the intensity of their happiness.

It even got to the point where I refused to criticize my children's mother even when she had obviously failed in some way. I wouldn't do it. And I wouldn't allow my children to criticize her either.

I'd tell them to quit making their mother's problems a big deal. I'd tell them their mother had gone through some tough experiences and that it was in times like these she needed their love and support more than ever. I would say that their mother was part of them, and for this reason they had to hold her in the highest respect. Their job was to love their mother.

What a complete change in direction for me. Here I was, discounting all her difficulties and taking a stand on her behalf.

How simple the method—how profound the results.

Finally I was heading in the right direction toward restoring the structural health my kids so desperately needed.

How simple the method—how profound the results.

CHANGES TAKING PLACE WITH THE MOM

Things were also changing for my ex.

I learned later that the good stories I was telling my kids about their mother were getting back to her. My kids were repeating everything I told them. As the stories held the mother in the most positive light, I guess she was learning that I was no longer an enemy.

What took place next surprised us all.

My daughter, now in her early twenties, rushed up to me one day, overjoyed. "Dad! Dad! The most incredible thing just happened. You're not going to believe this."

She told me she was sitting in a chair in her mother's bedroom just making idle talk with her mom when out of the blue her mother said something complimentary about me. Her mother told a story that held me in a good light. My daughter just sat there stunned, frozen in her chair, not moving a muscle, in total disbelief at what she was hearing.

For the first time in my daughter's conscious memory her mother said something kind about me.

For the first time in my daughter's conscious memory
her mother said something kind about me.

Spellbound, my daughter just sat there not saying a word, showing no positive reaction for fear that any affirmation on her part might turn the conversation back to something negative about me. So she forced herself to act as if everything was normal, as if complimenting her dad was something her mother did all the time.

But internally my daughter was so taken aback, so overcome with emotion, that she could hardly contain herself. She told me later that it was one of the most thrilling moments of her life.

Her mother's positive comment about me was nothing short of miraculous and my daughter knew it. Something was changing within her mother. And, my daughter felt something changing inside herself as well.

Something was changing within her mother. And,
my daughter felt something changing inside herself as well.

It was from that time forward that my daughter's mother ceased all negative words against me.

MERCY: THE TRANSFORMATION OF MY DAUGHTER

My daughter asked me, "Dad, do you remember all the times I've asked you why you and mom divorced?"

I thought to myself, do I remember? I'll never forget. Even though I had ceased speaking against my children's mother years earlier, that didn't stop my daughter from asking why we divorced. Every so often, up would come the question and I'd put her off by telling her that the reasons were just between her mother and me. Still, she kept trying to dig information out of me, and still, I'd give her the same answer.

So I said, "Yes, I remember."

"Well," my daughter said, "I don't need to ask you that question any longer." Then in almost hushed tones she added, "I know the answer. I understand my mom and I love my mom. She's still my mom and I still love her."

So that was it. Her question about why we divorced had somehow been answered and she never asked me that question again. Nor did I ask my daughter what she knew about why we divorced. Whatever it was, it satisfied her curiosity.

My daughter didn't know it at the time, but in her reply to me about her mother she had just hit the ignition switch and launched herself into incredible emotional health and stability.

She had just fulfilled Step 4: Mercy, and she fulfilled it perfectly.

...she had just hit the ignition switch and launched herself into incredible emotional health and stability.

Clearly knowing her mother's faults, clearly remembering the horrible difficulties of her past, my daughter chose to love her mother anyway.

In giving Mercy to her mom my daughter gave herself Mercy.

In ceasing her wars against her mother, she ceased all wars against herself.

Gone from inside my daughter was the dominance of her mother's criticisms and her mother's failures. Gone was the dominance of the pain in her past. Replaced within my daughter was this amazing Mercy.

The health that began to pour into my daughter was startling.

---

*In ceasing her wars against her mother,
she ceased all wars against herself.*

Once she began responding well toward her mother and me, nobody—not me, not my daughter, not anyone—could have predicted the changes that began to take place in her life.

The restoration of my daughter's internal structure accomplished more than anything we could have ever imagined.

My daughter found that she was released inside to step away from her difficult past.

---

*The restoration of my daughter's internal structure
accomplished more than anything we could have ever imagined.*

She began to think about consequences of her actions. She stopped wearing certain clothes, makeup, jewelry, piercings, and styles of hair. She stopped associating with certain people. She began making plans and setting goals. She began working regular hours and becoming a reliable and responsible employee. She spoke of starting college, owning a car, supporting herself, saving money, and being more careful with relationships.

The Principles and Steps were working.

FINALLY, MY FIRST SUCCESSFUL ENCOUNTER WITH MY EX

It only took me twenty years.

I had learned enough about the Two Principles and the Seven Steps to finally do what was formerly impossible for me to do.

My youngest son from my second marriage had joined the U.S. Marine Corps following high school and was about to graduate from basic training. We invited my ex and her youngest son—my son's best friend—to the USMC graduation and they came!

Leading up to the graduation I was wondering how it would go—being with my ex for two days.

I had anticipated some difficulties and prepared myself, but was surprised to find that things went great.

Instead of sitting apart from them, my wife and I spent our time with my ex and her son. I found in myself the ability to finally Accept my ex as a welcomed family member and for two days all of us were together during the graduation events and the final ceremony.

But, it was my ex who was the true hero. It was she who made the long, thirteen-hour drive, paying her own way, to see my son graduate. She was the one who was willing to be completely immersed in my family. And, because she cared for my son, my ex wore a T-Shirt which said, 'Marine Corps Mom.'

What a breakthrough for us. As far as I was concerned, our terrible past was put away. I was no longer under its dominating control. That day at my son's graduation I began a new life. From that time forward, seeing her and being with her became increasingly easy.

And, because she cared for my son, my ex wore a T-Shirt which said, 'Marine Corps Mom.'

Six months after my son graduated from boot camp, my ex's son also joined the Marines and graduated from the same Marine Corps boot camp. We were invited to join her family for his ceremonies. This time I was the one to make the long drive, take the time off work, pay my own expenses, and immerse myself in her family. I looked forward to the experience. My wife and I had a great time with my ex and her husband, honoring their son.

Before the afternoon graduation we were all gathered together with several thousand other parents and Marines at the large outdoor food court with multiple places to purchase food and to shop. We found a large table where we could all sit, followed by lively discussions about what to buy and what to eat. As plans progressed various people would leave to purchase food or wander through the many shops. I was becoming conscious of the fact that my ex and I just might be left alone at the table. And it happened. The last few individuals left leaving us sitting there across from each other.

I was surprised to find that I didn't mind at all.

It was weird but I felt okay and I found myself with the ability to talk normally and happily with her. Because of my understanding of the Two Principles and the Seven Steps, I knew exactly what I needed to do and why I needed to do it. And it made things go very well for us sitting alone together that sunny afternoon.

The Principles were now able to work without restraint—
one hundred percent positively—in our children's lives.

How strange our journey has been following our separation: twenty years of deep hatred for each other, our terrible criticisms, our bitter wars, the endless battles over the hearts and minds of our children, and the many years of cold silence. And now, here we are talking peacefully as if the years of conflicts and wars had never happened.

What a day! The benefits to our daughter and son that beautiful day in San Diego were life-changing.

The Principles were now able to work without restraint— one hundred percent positively—in our children's lives.

WHAT HAPPENED TO MY DAUGHTER?

At seventeen years of age my daughter met and married a young man who, like her, had problems. Together they had two children but their internal difficulties could not sustain a relationship, much less a marriage, and they divorced.

My daughter seized upon what we knew about the Principles and Steps, applying them to her own children and to her ex, preventing her children from experiencing the same Parent Wars that had so damaged her. What could have become a very toxic divorce that spelled disaster to her two kids became instead a peaceful separation. My daughter accepted her ex as critically important to her children's stability and maturity and saw to it that they remained very close to their father.

But what was also exciting to see was my daughter's own personal advancement into maturity.

As she responded well toward her mother and me, she found within herself the ability to become a more reliable and ambitious individual.

What could have become a very toxic divorce that spelled disaster to her two kids became instead a peaceful separation.

She took a minimum-wage job at a national company, working part-time on the graveyard shift serving customers at the counter. This was her first job after she began to repair internally.

That was over twelve years ago. Today my daughter is this

company's executive hiring manager for all of Southern California. She is responsible and hard-working and interacts easily among her friends and peers. She was recently flown to Dallas, Texas, by her company to attend a reception in her honor as one of two individuals selected among tens of thousands of employees to receive the Most Valuable Employee of the Year award. No one in her company has the slightest clue about her incredibly difficult past. Nor, do I imagine, would they ever believe that their executive employee was once completely incorrigible, self-emancipated at sixteen, and had spent time in a locked-down facility for troubled teens.

Today my daughter is in a wonderful second marriage and is living a life beyond her dreams. Her future plans are to attend law school in order to pursue her life ambition to become a family court judge.

Because of the Two Principles and Seven Steps the turnaround of my daughter has proven to be nothing short of miraculous.

My son too saw his own turnaround. Today he is married with a terrific family, is successful in his career, and is living life quite free from the twenty years of his parents at war.

WHAT ABOUT ME?

The transformation I sought for my children I found for myself.

I found a profound internal contentment that I never imagined existed. Peace with my ex and the incredible restoration of my children have given me relief beyond words.

But please don't misunderstand.

I don't want to give the impression that positive responses toward my ex are now simple and easy.

On the surface things may look good, yet deep within me I still have some unsettled heaviness that seems to linger like an old addiction.

But this has not prevented me from following the Two Principles and the Seven Steps.

It's just that in the future I would like to follow the rules without the accompanying internal resistance, unknown to anyone but me.

I don't know if that will ever happen.

Nevertheless, I will continue to press forward for the sake of my kids.

WE NEVER STOP LOOKING FOR OPPORTUNITIES

One summer weekend I took my son and some of his friends on a weekend road trip. Arriving home late Sunday afternoon I was very surprised to find my wife and my ex walking out our front door, with my ex holding a suitcase in her hand. My wife told me that my ex was just leaving.

My ex had spent the weekend in our home.

It turned out that she wanted to see our daughter who lived near us, but since there wasn't room for her to stay at our daughter's house, my wife had invited my ex to stay at our home.

I was surprised, to say the least. But I was also pleased to see my wife and my ex getting along so well together.

The best news, though, was my daughter so thoroughly benefiting from the care shown between her mother and step-mother.

Who would have ever thought that my ex would stay the weekend at my home?

It was early in December when I learned from my daughter that her mother was going to be by herself during the upcoming Christmas holiday as she and her husband were going through a separation.

My daughter and her family were joining us for Christmas dinner so I told her that her mother was also welcome to join us. In fact, my wife and I insisted that she come.

She accepted our invitation!

My ex would stay overnight at our daughter's house and come with my daughter and her family to our home on Christmas day.

As our Christmas dinners always included a lot of people, it would have been easy for me to bury myself in dinner preparations and conversation with other guests and have little to do with my ex. And nobody would have given it a thought if I arranged seating at the table so that we sat far apart. But this time I saw to it that she sat next to my wife and me at the head of the table.

There I was at Christmas dinner sitting for two hours next to my ex. I couldn't help but think about how this time of peace would penetrate deep into the internal framework of my children. Imagine the good it did for my daughter to see both her parents sitting together and enjoying each other's company.

And our older son, who is also in the Marine Corps and at the time was deployed overseas, certainly heard about our time together. How ironic. While at home in the United States, a country at peace, my son's entire life had been immersed with warring parents and internal conflicts. Now, in a foreign country filled with war, both structural halves within him were at peace.

A year later we invited my ex to the wedding of my youngest daughter (with my second wife) and were pleased that she came.

As I went around introducing my ex to my friends, no one could believe we got along so well. "This is your ex-wife?" they would ask—as if to say, "Aren't you supposed to hate each other?" Some of my friends had exes themselves and marveled at how we treated each other. They all told me I was so 'lucky.'

"This is your ex-wife?" they would ask—as if to say,
"Aren't you supposed to hate each other?"

I learned that evening that my ex was to fly to Spain the next morning and had planned on our daughter taking her to the airport. But since our daughter had some babysitting issues, I volunteered to drive.

Because of the late evening and the very early flight, my wife and I ended up with only two hours of sleep before driving five hours to get my ex to the airport and then return home.

Some people hearing this story have told me that I have taken Principle One a bit too far.

But I disagree.

I have well over twenty years of Parent Wars to make up to my kids.

---

*I have well over twenty years of Parent Wars
to make up to my kids.*

People don't know the depth of brokenness my kids suffered.

Nor do they understand that there is a dangerous natural tendency to fall back into old habits of blame and criticism—that I must continue practicing the Principles and Steps for the health of my children.

Driving my ex to the airport was an excellent opportunity to infuse Mercy and Benefit directly into the hearts of my now adult kids.

Knowing that every time I do something good for their mother it goes directly into strengthening my children's internal structures gives me incredible motivation. I must continue to move forward for their sakes.

I can't ever stop. I owe them so much.

So what are my plans now?

I think after writing this my wife and I will drive over to the town where my ex lives. There happen to be some nice restaurants there and I think we will invite my ex out to dinner. And we will invite her boyfriend along, too.

And we'll all enjoy ourselves.

And then I'll tell my kids.

AFTERWORD

Sitting with a group of separated parents who had all read PARENT WARS, one parent told us about a recent conversation she had with her ex.

Her ex had asked her to make a change in their daughter's schedule but she had told him no.

His response back to her was that his feelings were hurt because she didn't agree to the change.

The woman shook her head in disgust and said to us, "Can you believe this? How dare he talk to me about his 'feelings.' I wanted to say to him, 'You want to talk about hurt feelings? You want to go there? Who was the one who trashed our marriage? Who desecrated our vows? Who caused our daughter and me months of anguish and grief? Who forced us to move out of our beautiful home? Whose lives were completely shattered? How dare you tell me your feelings are hurt because I didn't give in to one of your trivial requests.'"

But, the woman said, she didn't go there.

Instead, she simply told her ex that she was going to stay with her decision anyway, and ended their conversation.

She said to us that prior to reading this book she and her ex would have gotten into a huge argument over his ridiculous 'hurt' feelings. But now she's decided that it's time to have better responses for the sake of their daughter.

Everyone in the group admired this woman for not getting into a shouting match with her ex, but the mom just shrugged it off. She didn't think what she did was any big deal.

But this book disagrees.

This mom's response was a *huge deal*.

She began!

She began the journey toward restoration in herself and her daughter.

For the first time since her separation the mother stepped away from her difficult past. Instead of linking this latest issue to a thousand other issues she's had with her ex, she kept everything in the present—in the moment—only dealing with the issue at hand.

And, if she continues, this mom and her daughter will experience—as I and scores of other separated parents have—the remarkable transformation brought about by these life-changing Principles and Steps.

THE TWO PRINCIPLES

Principle One: *What parents do to each other, they do directly to their kids.*

Principle Two: *What children do to their parents, they do directly to themselves.*

THE SEVEN STEPS

Step 1: Understanding is to acknowledge that children are half mother and half father. Therefore, both biological parents—living or deceased, in their children's lives or not—will always be keys to the emotional health of their children and must be given considerable respect.

Step 2: Acceptance means that you are to accept life as it is now handed to you. It means to Accept your separation, the fact that you now have an ex, and the reality that your children are going to be raised between two households. It means to Accept your ex's partner, the partner's children and family, and to allow them, with safeguards in place, into your life and your children's lives.

Step 3: Amnesia means to put away the *negative emotions* of the past, and to treat the other parent as if there has never been a problem between you. Amnesia is to never inform your children of the difficulties you have suffered because of their other parent.

Step 4: Mercy is recognizing a parent's failures but adding a *but*, *still*, *yet*, or *nevertheless*, followed by expressions of care and love for that parent. Children are not designed to measure out justice or issue verdicts or penalties toward their own parents: They are only designed to give them Mercy.

Step 5: Neutral—Damaging recognizes that only positive responses between parents, and positive responses between children and parents, build stable internal structures in children.

Any other kind of response—Neutral or negative—will continue to damage kids.

Step 6: Benefiting means to do good to the ex and the ex's new family, now! It's setting the example for your children. It's behaving as if you are healed from your difficult past with your ex.

Step 7: The Cost of Doing Business is *adapting* to the difficult behaviors of the other parent and *enduring* hardship. It also means *making* peace for the sake of the stability of your kids.

ACKNOWLEDGMENTS

Words cannot express my appreciation to my daughter and son for their amazing transparency in allowing their stories to be told and for their input and critique of this book. Great appreciation goes to my wife, Jenetha, for her encouragement, incredible patience, and incomparable expertise in content editing. Recognition goes also to our seven adult children who watched with interest the progression and development of this book—thank you. Thanks also to my mother, Dr. Elizabeth Glenn, for her expert editing and enthusiastic belief in the ideas presented here.

Special thanks to Dan Benson for his copy editing. Thanks to Ron Macciola and Laura Taggart, M.A., for their helpful critiques and suggestions. Special thanks to G. Miller Hogan II, J.D., and Jonathan Kirsch, J.D., for their professional reviews and book vetting. Thanks to Nash Jafri of Designior for creating five great illustrations. Thanks to Alan Gadney and Carolyn Porter of One-on-One Book Production and Marketing for an excellent interior book design. Thanks, again, to Alan Gadney for offering expert marketing advice. And thanks to Bo Lane for a terrific book cover.

ABOUT DR. DONALD R. PARTRIDGE

The author's children were two and five years old when his first marriage of twelve years ended.

Two years later Don married Jenetha who was divorced with three children. Together they had two more children bringing the total number of kids in their family to seven.

For the first two decades of their marriage they suffered through the difficult wars with the author's ex and heartbreaking issues with his children.

Understanding personally the complex problems experienced by separated parents and their children, Don and Jenetha decided that Don would change careers. After earning his graduate degrees he immersed himself full-time in issues common to separated parents.

In his work it became clear to the author that few children come out of their parents' separations emotionally intact. What also became clear were solutions in the form of several key Principles and Steps which are critical to the restoration of children following parent separation.

This book represents over a decade of practicing these Principles and Steps and observing their amazing benefit to the author's own family and to separated-parent families throughout the country.

Dr. Partridge has written eight books for separated parents, is a radio commentator (over 200 radio shows), and is an avid public speaker and workshop host providing leading-edge information for single parents and stepfamilies nationwide.

HOW TO ORDER ADDITIONAL COPIES

Give the gift of PARENT WARS to your relatives,
friends, and colleagues—and to your ex!

To order, go online to www.pearpublishing.net. Or write:

Pear Publishing, Inc.
PO Box 10092
Pleasanton, CA 94588-2747

Contact Pear Publishing, Inc. if you are interested in scheduling Dr. Donald Partridge and/or his daughter as a speaker.

For companies or non-profit organizations interested in purchasing books for resale, information about discounts and quantity purchases is available at www.pearpublishing.net.